SCRIPTWRITING

SCRIPTWRITING

UEA MA
Creative Writing Anthologies
2021

CONTENTS

TILLY LUNKEN	Foreword	VII
STEVE WATERS	Introduction	IX
ALLY ARTUCH	High Home	2
LACEY AUSTIN	Goodbye, Ethel	12
DAN CLARK	Mrs Roberts	20
JENNIFER COLLARD	Putri Kemuning	32
ROSA COOPER-DAVIES	Supply	44
JACK FAIREY	Every Seven Years	58
SEBASTIAN GARBACZ	A Love Letter to All Those Who Care About Jack	72
SAM GILLETT	Love Underground	80
KATEY HOFFMAN	Angelfish	92
MEHMET IZBUDAK	Evening Walk	100
IMOGEN LEA	Bed-In	110
HATTIE MANTON	King Size	120
LOUISE PESERY	Woman	128
ROSALIE PRATT	Angle	136
LINDSAY SHARMAN	But What Did They Actually Do?	148
HUGHIE SHEPHERD-CROSS	The Beholder	158
ALEX VINEY	Gender Rolls: "The Purple Dress"	168
ALEXANDER WISEMAN	There's A Hole in My Bucket	178
YU CHING WONG	Lie Detectors	188
	Acknowledgements	197

TILLY LUNKEN

Foreword

Reflection. It's what writing does. It looks backwards, forwards, inside and out. It distorts or reveals truth, but it contains in essence part of us. As a writer and a reader. Who we are informs how we receive it, how we craft it. It can be a revelation.

The writing I have done most this past year has been entirely for myself. I began journalling at the start of lockdown 1.0 and have continued it as a daily practice since. What interests me as much about this practice as a record, a diary, a witness, as therapy – is that there is no audience. It isn't for anyone else but me. In fact, it is for me before anyone else. Sure, as an artist I have an awareness that it might get used at some point but actually, if it doesn't – that doesn't diminish its importance.

What we have here, of course, is a collection of writing that is for an audience and what a treat it is. I didn't get to meet this cohort in person – but meeting them through the pages of this anthology has been a delight – and revealing.

Once again, it is impossible to write this without the context of the past year, where most teaching has been online. To those not on the front line of the pandemic, it's as if time exists differently – some of us even stopped. Ultimately, I think we've all changed. Thematically all these pieces involve choice – a moment, a beginning, a change and a point where there is no return. An anthology of reflections and refractions.

An angelfish – both trapped and free, the sheer joy of the B-side you are sure no one else has discovered, and the moment you see your younger self in the life you will soon dress your own daughter in. A centaur forced into a new suit, a small child forced onto a train clutching her favourite toy and a plate of carrots drops over and over again – before reality breaks through.

A teacher daydreams of consequences and a boy comes to understand them through an unexpected and tempting ally. The train is coming, it's really coming – it's really coming, but up on the roof no one can really know how drunk you need to be to stop caring. Dating apps really do age you, right? But who would want to choose a relationship when you can't even figure out buckets together or finish the easy crossword? There's meaning in the marks on the walls, the way the river slips by and through London and in the glance over to a beautiful dress and the promise of a different life. Everyone is a liar though, that's the truth of it and of course everything crystallises in an art gallery.

Nineteen pieces. Little windows to peek through and enjoy, also catching a glimpse of ourselves in the glass.

And so a little reflection.

What you write, however you write, and whoever you write it for – know that you exist beyond an audience. You might this year have co-written an anthology, drafted dissertation scripts over a stormy summer, learned about radio drama and built up a strong toolkit for screenwriting. You also might have twelve full Moleskine journals (no lines, never lines) that contain the most important writing you'll ever do and have accepted that perhaps no one will ever read it.

How is it August again? How am I again sitting in my room listening to *folklore* and thinking once more of my time at UEA?

In my mind I can trace the pathway from Norfolk Terrace to the laundry, carrying my big bag of washing. Buying snacks at the Union Shop to get coins/change and skimping on the dryer, but always doing at least one turn as the weight of sodding washing was not worth it. I can feel the reality of that, and now as I walk down my stairs, less than 20m with my green washing tub, I think of the weight of other things too. The layers of our lives and experience and how we break down, build and grow. How we recover. How we remember. I think of the boy I showed how to use the top loader in freshers' week and saw weeks later throwing his washing in like a pro.

I don't know. This year. Change. Choice. It happens when we are stuck inside. It happens when we look out and look in. Reflect. Write. And read.

Inside these pages, I hope you find as much as I have.

STEVE WATERS

Introduction

Writing in the Dark

It's a great pleasure to introduce this anthology of writing by this year's cohort of MA Scriptwriters – perhaps more so than usual, as these writers have kept their imaginations alive in one of the most difficult years imaginable. During this year of lockdowns, quarantines and new viral variants, keeping going has required courage, tenacity – and talent. Thankfully, these 20 writers have these qualities in abundant supply. But what's more interesting is the way in which these dark times have ignited their imagination – nothing's taken for granted in these pages, neither form, content, nor identity itself. Perhaps, in a year of closed theatres and cancelled films, drama itself has become more precious and stranger to us.

Some of the works here frankly acknowledge those restrictions; Mehmet Izbudak's looks humanely at a couple navigating the long days of lockdown and Imogen Lea's fractured 'Bed-In' examines how time itself buckles under their formlessness. Closely observed relationships reveal the insight and maturity of much of the writing here, whether in Alexander Wiseman's comic and wry anatomy of longing or Jack Fairey's profanely charming evocation of teenagers becoming friends in 'Every Seven Years'. And is it fanciful to see Sam Gillett's thrillingly funny audit of rave culture in 'Love Underground' as a hymn to freedoms lost?

These tales of love, need and community span the world from Jennifer Collard's moving examination of arranged marriage in Indonesia to Hattie Manton's hair-curlingly frank dissection of mid-life female sexuality in 'King Size'. Everywhere, fault lines of gender and desire bring an electric charge to relationships, whether in the Louvre Gallery where, in Louise Pesery's 'Woman', lovers break up in front of a painting, or in the mayhem of a late-night party in Rosalie Pratt's near wordless short film 'Angle'. And there's little sentiment about female solidarity to be found in Lindsay Sharman's devastating tale of single-sex bullying, 'But What Did They Actually Do?'

And nor are these writers content to limit themselves to realism; strange times demand that form itself is challenged. Ally Artuch reaches for fable in her comic but troubling exploration of gentrification in 'High Home' and Yu Ching Wong fashions an allegory of daily deceit in 'Lie Detectors'. Hughie Shepherd-Cross travels from social comedy to the surreal in his Pinteresque 'The Beholder'; Sebastian Garbacz's intense radio monologue blurs event and inner experience and, more playfully, Rosa Cooper-Davies's 'Supply' puts a fantasist teacher through his paces.

Desire and feeling transform what we see and feel in most of the film work here – Dan Clark's 'Mrs Roberts' nightmarishly captures the confusions of delusion; more tenderly Alex Viney uses the mayhem of Dungeons and Dragons as a lens to look at a longing to change gender. So often these writers side with those at the edge of life: in Lacey Austin's 'Goodbye, Ethel', we see war and evacuation through a child's eyes; and in Katey Hoffman's heartbreaking 'Angelfish', an abortion clinic is dispassionately scrutinised by a young woman.

As I write, some sort of post-pandemic world is struggling to be born – but this collection of dramas in all media from across the world reveals how even in the most constrained times, great writing can – and must – flourish. I hope this anthology is one portent of better days to come for all of us.

Steve Waters, Professor of Scriptwriting, July 2021

SCRIPTWRITING

HIGH HOME

(A short script)

Written by

Ally Artuch

Ally Artuch was born and raised in the Cayman Islands before moving to the UK for university. She achieved her BA in English Literature at the University of East Anglia before pursuing her MA in Creative Writing: Scriptwriting.

allyartuch@gmail.com

FADE IN:

EXT. HIGH HOME VILLAGE — CONTINUOUS

Rohan, a centaur (50s), trots along a dirt path. He passes by a few wooden cottages with sprawling overgrown front gardens.

He continues on, passing more cottages and waving at the other centaurs passing by. Everywhere is luscious green. A few centaur children race past him, cantering down the path. He laughs.

INT. ROHAN'S CAVE — DAY

The sun is setting. Rohan sits in a sparsely decorated cave lighting a fire. A flame sparks and he picks up a coin purse and begins to count.

A strange noise from outside catches his attention. Hesitantly, he stands up and makes his way to the cave entrance.

In front of him, a faun (Hawthorn) and an elf (Dione) are walking up the hill towards his cave. Each are wearing formal, well-tailored suits and the faun is holding a briefcase. They spot Rohan and move closer.

                    ROHAN
          What is that you're wearing?

The faun sighs, as if expecting this question. He turns to look at the elf, disgruntled.

                    HAWTHORN
          Honestly, you really do forget how
          far behind these shithole villages
          are from the city. 'What are you
          wearing?' That has to be the ninth
          time someone's asked us this today.

Rohan's eyes widen in surprise. The elf clears his throat.

                    DIONE
          I'm sorry, Mr...

                    ROHAN
      Rohan.

                    DIONE
          Rohan. My partner and I have had a
          long day, please excuse him. I am Mr
          Dione and this is Mr Hawthorn; we
          come from Aldea City and to answer
          your question, we are wearing Mrs
          Nightshade's finest, tailor-made
          suits. One of the perks of the job.
          Do you mind if we speak with you
          inside your... er, cave?

Rohan does not speak. He stares, completely baffled. Hawthorn steps inside and pushes past Rohan. Dione clears his throat again and adjusts his tie. He smiles, embarrassed, before moving in.

Rohan follows after them. Looking around the main chamber Hawthorn looks unimpressed.

The cave walls are covered with drawings carved into the stone. There are images of centaurs hunting, farming and gathering together. There is a makeshift bed made from a pile of knitted blankets against the back wall. Next to the blankets is a deep chest. The fire is crackling in the centre of the room, with a cast-iron kettle placed next to it.

                    HAWTHORN
          Quaint.

                    ROHAN
          Oh, please, sit down.

Rohan gestures towards the ground. There are no chairs.

                    DIONE
          I think it might be better if we
          stand. Besides, we shouldn't be too
          long.

                    ROHAN
          All right... Would you at least like
          some tea? The brew is an old family
          recipe.

                    DIONE
          Yes please, that is very kind of
          you. Thank you.

Dione looks pointedly at Hawthorn.

                    HAWTHORN
          Yeah, sure.

Rohan busies himself making the tea. He opens the chest and takes out three worn teacups.

                    ROHAN
          Do either of you like milk? There
          are a few goats that live on the
          land out here.

Rohan looks over at Hawthorn who looks offended.

                    HAWTHORN
          Just because I'm a faun doesn't mean
          I drink goat's milk.

                    DIONE
          I think just sugar will be fine,
          thank you.

Rohan sheepishly continues setting up the drinks and avoids Hawthorn's gaze. Eventually he hands the two piping hot teacups over.

                    DIONE (CONT'D)
          So, as I was saying, Rohan, my
          colleague and I have travelled a
          long way to get here and I'm afraid
          we have some, er, unfortunate news.

                    ROHAN
          What is it?

                    DIONE
          This cave, your home, we're afraid
          to inform you that you are living
          here... illegally.

                    ROHAN
          I don't understand.

Hawthorn sighs in frustration and pinches the bridge of his nose.

HAWTHORN
Rohan, listen. We've had this exact conversation with almost all of the creatures here at High Home, so I'll just be blunt. The land that you're living on, right here, is owned by King Thaddeus. You have no right to be here. You are actually committing a crime by living here.

Rohan
(confused)
But my family have always lived here. This was my mother and father's cave before they passed. My ancestors have lived in these woods for hundreds of years.

DIONE
Yes, we understand that this village has been inhabited by centaurs for a very long time now, but the thing is, your ancestors were also living here illegally. The King owns all the land, and now he has big plans for High Home, which is why we're here.

Hawthorn opens up his briefcase and hands Rohan a sheet of paper. It is a projected photo of a built-up high street, full of lots of coffee shops, vintage clothing stores and flats.

HAWTHORN
Pretty cool, right? You see, our data analysis has been showing an increased desire from Aldea City residents to move further out into the countryside. It's understandable of course, crime rates are going up, families want to settle down...

DIONE
Our analytics placed High Home village as the optimal spot for relocating city residents. Lots of open space, less pollution. It's perfect.

                    HAWTHORN
          Anyway, we need you to sign this.

Hawthorn hands Rohan another sheet of paper but offers
no explanation. Dione takes a sip of his tea and nods
appreciatively.

                    ROHAN
               (embarrassed)
          I can't read.

                    DIONE
          It's an agreement where you
          acknowledge that King Thaddeus
          rightfully owns the land that you
          currently occupy. By signing you are
          forfeiting your right to occupancy
          of this land.

                    ROHAN
          But where will I live?

                    DIONE
          We'll be building some temporary
          housing for current residents of
          High Home, for at least until they
          can get back on their feet — sorry,
          hooves — and find appropriate
          accommodation for themselves.

                    HAWTHORN
          But Rohan, buddy, listen. Your cave
          here is just a little out of the way
          of High Home. Between the three of
          us, it's pretty unlikely that anyone
          will build anything here right away.
          You'll get to live here for a few
          more years.

                    DIONE
          We just need you to sign the form
          on the off-chance that someone does
          decide to build on this land.

Rohan looks at the paper once more.

                    ROHAN
          And what if I don't sign this?

DIONE
Well, that would be worst case scenario and you would be in quite some trouble. You'd need a lawyer, which would be a total waste of money because you'd lose the legal battle, and we would repossess your cave. By signing this now, you'll at least be able to keep all of your possessions and savings.

Dione grabs a pen from his front pocket and holds it out for Rohan.

HAWTHORN
Come on, Rohan. Sign the paper. Everyone else has, you're our last stop.

After a few moments, Rohan grabs the pen.

EXT. HIGH HOME VILLAGE — DAY

Rohan clops along the same dirt path. He slows down as he nears a cottage in the process of being torn down.

In the garden stands a group of dwarves wearing hard hats and high-visibility vests. Rohan stares at them curiously.

CONSTRUCTION DWARF
What are you looking at, horse face?

All of the dwarves laugh. Rohan ignores them and continues through the village, passing by more and more groups of construction workers.

CUT TO:

INT. ROHAN'S CAVE — DAY

Rohan wakes up with a start as a loud horn blasts from outside of his cave.

CONSTRUCTION DWARF
(through a speaker)
Please exit the cave!

He moves towards the entryway. Outside the cave stands a
large construction crew. One dwarf stands in front, holding a
megaphone.

                   CONSTRUCTION DWARF (CONT'D)
    Get your bags, horse, we've got work
    to do.

Rohan sighs in defeat before turning around back towards his
cave. Once out of view, the head construction dwarf speaks to
his friends and Rohan stops.

                   CONSTRUCTION DWARF (CONT'D)
    Fuckin' hate centaurs. Disgusting
    creatures, they are. Think they can
    shit anywhere they like, especially
    out here in these rural areas where
    they ain't got no fouling laws.
    Smells worse than the city. And I
    thought fauns were uncivilised.
    Watch where you step, fellas.

Rohan moves further into his cave. The fire is out. He grabs
his pile of knitted blankets and dumps them into a chest.
Rohan looks around the cave walls one last time. He is drawn
towards a carving of three centaurs: a male, female and their
child all holding hands. He places his hand on top of the
drawings, tracing over them. After a few moments, Rohan turns
away and grabs the chest. His possessions clink loudly inside.

EXT. HIGH HOME VILLAGE — MOMENTS LATER

Rohan clops on the now paved road through High Home,
struggling to carry the chest. Most of the old wooden
cottages have now been transformed into small shops and
cafés.

He passes a pub called The Dragon's Den and continues past a
few fast-food restaurants. The trees are gone. High Home is
almost entirely unrecognisable.

INT. HIGH HOME TEMPORARY HOUSING DAY ROOM — DAY

Rohan is knitting. His large body makes the room feel
cramped. There is a small television in the corner where
a stand-up comedian is performing. Two young centaurs sit
nearby, fighting over a video game.

                    STAND-UP COMEDIAN
          So, I was on the bus the other day
          and you know what I saw? I saw a
          centaur trying to squeeze its fat
          beep into one of them seats ahead
          of me and it got me thinking. Why do
          centaurs take public transport in
          the first place? Just beeping run.

The audience laughs. Rohan stops knitting and looks at the TV.

                    STAND-UP COMEDIAN (CONT'D)
          No, I'm being serious right, like
          they're part horse. They are the
          transport!

Rohan puts his knitting needles down. He stands and immediately knocks over the coffee table — including a mug of tea on top of it. The children stop arguing.

Rohan walks towards the door. He has to hunch so as not to hit the ceiling.

                    STAND-UP COMEDIAN (CONT'D)
          Centaurs are so—

                                                  CUT TO:

EXT. HIGH HOME VILLAGE — CONTINUOUS

Rohan takes up almost all of the pavement. There is a small build-up of traffic along the road, moving steadily. A few passers-by shoot him dirty looks as they step into the road to move past him.

A centaur in compression shorts and an athletic top canters past on the road, pulling along an elf and a faun in a rickshaw. Dione and Hawthorn. They are laughing and enjoying themselves. Rohan stops and watches them move away.

A tinkering of a bell captures his attention. He looks three shops down to see a door to a coffee shop being opened. He heads towards it.

EXT/INT. KAPPA'S KOFFEE KAFÉ — DAY

The sign out front of the shop reads 'Kappa's Koffee Kafé'.

Rohan grabs the doorknob and pushes the door open. The barista at the counter looks up and blushes, clearly embarrassed.

> BARISTA
> Oh, uh, I'm sorry, sir. We don't have enough space for you in here. We're working on a back entrance for centaurs. It'll be finished in a couple of months.

The customers all stop talking to stare. A group of teenage elves begin to giggle.

> TEENAGE ELF
> (whispering loudly)
> He's not wearing any clothes!

EXT. HIGH HOME VILLAGE — CONTINUOUS

Rohan exits the café and keeps walking, passing The Dragon's Den pub. After several minutes, he nears a newly constructed area. He walks towards a hill, the same one leading to his old cave.

At the top of the hill where his home once was stands a shop. Mrs Nightshade's Tailored Suits.

INT. MRS NIGHTSHADE'S TAILORED SUITS — DAY

The walls are bare and painted crimson. The shop is lined with mannequins dressed in expensive suits. Two leather sofas rest against the back wall. There is a velvet curtain blocking off the dressing rooms. The sales assistant — a smartly dressed elf — looks up from the till.

> SALES ASSISTANT
> Is there anything I can help you with, sir?

> ROHAN
> Yes... I would like to buy a suit.

FADE OUT.

THE END

GOODBYE, ETHEL

(A short script extract)

Written by

Lacey Austin

Lacey Austin is an aspiring scriptwriter with an interest in writing for screen. She enjoys writing scripts in the gothic genre, more specifically, writing horror/supernatural, dark romance, fantasy and period screenplays. She has a BA in Scriptwriting and Performance and will complete her MA in Scriptwriting in 2021.

laceyaustinscripts@yahoo.com

The faint sound of music is coming from a radio.

FADE IN ON:

INT. EVAN'S FAMILY BATHROOM — 1939 — NIGHT

A dull, cramped bathroom. ETHEL EVANS (8) is in the bath. Water cascades over her head, over her delicate features.

Her mother, Maggie (30s), sleeves rolled up, leans on her knees over the edge. She gathers bath water in a small cup.

> MAGGIE
> Come on, Ethel, tip your head back more, close your eyes...

Ethel does so and Maggie gently pours the water over Ethel's head again.

Suddenly, the music stops — the radio hisses, crackles — and a sharp, abrupt VOICE emerges over the static:

> RADIO VOICE (V.O.)
> We interrupt this programme to bring you an important announcement from the Government. Operation Pied Piper is among us. Our streets are threatened, our children must flee—

The radio is switched off. We hear no more...

One of Ethel's eyes squints open, sees her mother kneel back down beside the bath, teary-eyed.

> MAGGIE
> Keep your eyes closed Ethel. You don't want to get soap in them...

Ethel closes her eyes again. Maggie scoops up more water and continues to pour it over Ethel's head...

INT. ETHEL'S BEDROOM — NIGHT

Curtains drawn. A dim table light is on.

Ethel, wet hair combed back, dressed in a nightgown, sits cross-legged on the floor. She hums a little tune to herself as she plays with her dolls. Mr Tumbolt, her scruffy teddy, is in her lap.

As she plays, Ethel looks up, watches her mother flit around the bedroom, packing things into a SMALL SUITCASE.

A SCARY-LOOKING MASK with big holes for EYES and a LARGE CIRCULAR MOUTH rests on the cabinet by the open suitcase.

CUT TO:

INT. ETHEL'S BEDROOM — LATER

The bed quilt is thrown back. Ethel clambers into bed with Mr Tumbolt. Maggie tucks her in.

                    MAGGIE
Come on, let's tuck you in...

                    ETHEL
And Mr Tumbolt too.

                    MAGGIE
And Mr Tumbolt too. Can't have him going cold now, can we? We've got to tuck you in tight, so the bed bugs don't—

                    ETHEL
Are we going on holiday, Mummy?

Maggie falters. She doesn't know what to say. Sits down on the edge of the bed. Thinks for a moment...or two. Gathers herself.

                    MAGGIE
Something like that.

                    ETHEL
Can Mr Tumbolt come too?

Maggie smiles a little, gently tucks a strand of hair behind Ethel's ear.

                    MAGGIE
Yes, Mr Tumbolt can come too.

                          ETHEL
                Where are we going?

Maggie stiffens, looks away from Ethel, places Mr Tumbolt
under the blanket.

                          MAGGIE
                Don't you worry about that, right
                now, darling —
                     (pulls blanket higher)
                You... and Mr Tumbolt need to get
                some sleep.

Ethel looks up at her mother, notices something:

                          ETHEL
                Mummy, are you crying? What's wrong?

                          MAGGIE
                No... no of course not. Mummy's
                just... Mummy's fine.
                     (clears throat)
                Right, you. Enough talk. Get some
                rest...

Maggie leans in close, kisses Ethel's forehead gently.
Without another word, Maggie straightens up, moves off the
bed, towards the door.

Ethel watches her go.

Just before she leaves, Maggie turns back — face obscured
by the semi-darkness of the room. Her voice trembles as she
speaks.

                          MAGGIE
                Goodnight, sweetie.

And with that, she leaves, shutting the door quietly behind
her.

We see, from the thin gap at the bottom of the door, Maggie's
shadow linger a moment, then disappear.

Ethel turns on her side, Mr Tumbolt in her arms, staring over
at the door... At her suitcase.

That horrible mask set on top, its HUGE, GHASTLY SHADOW over
the door.

She swallows hard, squeezes Mr Tumbolt a little tighter, then not wanting to see the mask or the suitcase anymore, she quickly reaches out, switches off the table light and we fall into —

DARKNESS.

Which, along with a horrible silence, remains for the longest of moments and then we hear it.

A FAINT SOUND rising over the darkness.

A WHISTLING.

Growing louder and louder until...

The SHRILL, PIERCING SCREAM of a TRAIN'S WHISTLE becomes so loud in our ears, we immediately —

CUT TO:

INT. WATERLOO TRAIN STATION — DAY

The train whistle continues.

A PAIR OF HEELS and a small pair of MARY JANES rush through the busy platform, through the throng of a thousand feet.

Flustered, Maggie drags Ethel through the growing crowd of PARENTS and CHILDREN as a HUGE STEAM TRAIN pulls into the station. The crowd bustles forward.

                    MAGGIE
          Come on, Ethel, we have to find your
          compartment.

Ethel falls behind, Mr Tumbolt dangling by her side. A SMALL GAS MASK BOX hangs over her shoulder and bounces up and down as she hurries.

She stares at the whirl of people around her. At parents saying goodbye to their children as they board the train. Train conductors yell at the top of their lungs, tossing luggage into carriages. People flood from all directions, pushing and shoving towards the train. Voices swirl all around.

It's chaotic. Everything spins. Ethel falls behind and lets go of her mother's hand.

                    MAGGIE
              (looking back)
Ethel, come on. We can't mess around, we've got to find your compartment.

                    ETHEL
Mummy, I don't like this...

                    MAGGIE
              (rushes back to Ethel)
You'll be fine...
              (takes Ethel's hand)
You and Mr Tumbolt are going on an adventure.

Maggie pulls Ethel through the shifting crowd, craning her head to look at the compartments.

                    ETHEL
But we don't want to go...

                    MAGGIE
Don't be silly...

                    ETHEL
Mummy, we don't want to go!

                    MAGGIE
              (sharply, turning around)
Ethel, please! You've got to.

Ethel freezes, taken back... stares up at her mother. Maggie's immediately apologetic.

                    MAGGIE
Oh darling, I'm sorry...
              (kneels before Ethel)
It's not as simple as that.
              (pause)
Do you remember Mummy telling you things would get a little... strange for a while?
              (off Ethel's NOD)
And that I'd need you to be brave when things did? Well...

                    TRAIN CONDUCTOR (O.S.)
          Train's leaving in a minute, ma'am.
          Time to say your goodbyes.

Ethel peers up, sees a TRAIN CONDUCTOR towering beside them. He eyes her, then looks to Maggie. Her mother forces a smile, nods, then hands him the suitcase. Ethel glances back at her mother, confused.

Maggie begins to straighten her hat. Fix her collar.

                    MAGGIE
          Now, I need you to be a big, brave
          girl for Mummy, OK? Do you think you
          can do that? Can you do that for me,
          Ethel?

Ethel's sad eyes meet her mother's.

Then almost instantly, Maggie throws her arms around Ethel squeezing her tight. It's a long embrace. Neither want to let go.

The TRAIN ENGINE hisses — a loud GUST of SMOKE.

                    TRAIN CONDUCTOR
               (calling out)
          Final call. That's the final call.
          All children aboard.

Maggie pulls away, touches Ethel's cheek tenderly. It's the final hurry...

                    MAGGIE
               (over the train whistle)
          Right, you've got your gas mask...
          name badge... Mr Tumbolt — you're all
          set.
               (kisses Ethel's cheek)
          Goodbye, darling.

Maggie rises, stands back. Nods to the train conductor who now stands beside them. He places a tender hand on Ethel's shoulder, starts to steer her towards the carriage, through the crowd.

Ethel is completely bewildered, it's happening all too quickly.

                    ETHEL
                (confused)
            Mummy?

                    MAGGIE
                (calling out)
            I love you, sweetie.

                    ETHEL
            Mummy... aren't you coming with me?

                    MAGGIE
            It's OK, darling... off you go. Go with
            the nice man, he'll look after you.

                    ETHEL
            I don't want him. I want you,
            Mummy... Mummy... Mummy! What's going
            on?

The train conductor ushers her onto the busy carriage full of children.

As the conductor gets on, the TRAIN lets out another gust of steam.

Ethel quickly turns to look back at the platform.

Her face falls.

She cranes her head a little... tries to SEE...

Mr Tumbolt falls limply by her side.

Her mother has already GONE. Disappeared in the crowd of a thousand faces...

                    ETHEL
                (quietly, to herself)
            Mummy?

And as the train doors close on her. Cut to:

BLACKOUT.

MRS ROBERTS

Written by

Dan Clark

Dan Clark is a screenwriter from Norwich, primarily
specialising in short film, sit-com and the occasional
radio drama. Although his list of professional work is
short and unimpressive, he's currently developing a short
radio play with BBC veteran Jeremy Mortimer, and is under
mentorship from professional screenwriter Jude Tindall
(*Shakespeare & Hathaway*).

danclark1999@gmail.com

1   INT. DINING ROOM — NIGHT

ELLA ROBERTS, 28, leans against the counter of a 1960s kitchen, smoking through a cigarette holder. She gazes out of a window, smiling at the snow as it falls outside.

A sharp *ding* cuts through the calm.

						ELLA
			Oh bugger.

She wheels around, shimmying to the oven and pulling it open, recoiling as smoke pours out of the door. She wafts it away, grabbing a pair of oven gloves and pulling out a tray of carrots.

She whisks round to the counter and pours the carrots onto a silver platter.

2   INT. HALLWAY — NIGHT

Ella struts down a hallway, carrots in hand.

Warm light and the sound of a piano oozes out of a doorway at the end of the hall. A dinner party. A booming laugh carries out of the room. Ella smiles and rolls her eyes.

Suddenly, the light from the doorway flicks off, the hallway dropping into darkness.

The piano and laughter fades away, the alien sound of television static filling the scene.

Ella's face floods with confusion, the TV static growing louder and louder.

She picks up the pace, her high-heeled feet bouncing across the carpet.

Ella fumbles the carrots, the platter crashing to the floor. She leaves them behind, desperately stumbling to the door.

3   INT. DINING ROOM — NIGHT

The rest of the Robertses sit around a grand dining table, the surface covered in candelabras, cutlery and Christmas dinner. A Christmas tree stands in the corner, tall enough to brush the ceiling.

EDDIE, 28, sits at a piano in the corner of the room, dressed in a tweed suit. Drunk, he taps away at Christmas songs, sporadically hitting the wrong notes. We see only the back of his head.

JACK, 60s, leans on his elbows, puffing away at a cigar. He glares at the back of Eddie's head.

Eddie hits a wrong note.

                    JACK
     If you're not gonna play it right,
     don't bother.

AGGIE, 80s, slaps Jack's shoulder with a gloved hand.

                    AGGIE
     Leave the boy alone, Jack. I think
     he's marvellous.

                    JACK
     Not at the piano.

Ella bursts into the room, face full of horror.

                  JACK (CONT'D)
     Finally! What took you so long?

                    ELLA
     Oh um—

Ella looks back at the hallway, frowning. She looks over her family, confused.

                  ELLA (CONT'D)
     I dropped the carrots.

                    AGGIE
     You're holding the carrots dear.

Ella looks down to her hands, jumping slightly as she realises she's still holding the silver platter.

                    JACK
     The girl's lost the bleeding plot.

                    AGGIE
     Jack!

                    ELLA
          Sorry, might've had one too many.

                    JACK
          You and your husband. He's in
          another world over there.

Ella looks to Eddie, still fumbling away on the piano.

                    ELLA
          He's still learning. Trying to get
          in with the church choir.

                    AGGIE
          How splendid!

                    JACK
          He's got a long way to go.

Ella walks around the side of the table, placing the carrots in the centre of the spread.

                    ELLA
          Where's Mummy?

                    JACK
          She's popped to the loo. Said we
          should start without her.

                    AGGIE
          She most certainly did not.

                    JACK
          Oh, you know Ruth. She wouldn't want
          us to go hungry. Grub up!

                    ELLA
          Your funeral.

Ella walks to her seat at the head of the table, stroking Eddie's shoulder as she passes.

                    ELLA (CONT'D)
          Dad, I've been meaning to ask Mum
          about New Year's. Do you want to
          have it here or at yours?

Jack looks at his daughter, perplexed.

                    JACK
          Decisions like that are above my pay
          grade. Ask her yourself.

He motions across the table, revealing RUTH, 60s, the
matriarch now magically sitting across from him, filling
the previously empty seat in front of the carrots.

The TV static returns, Ella wincing and grabbing at her
forehead. Eddie hits a wrong note on the piano.

                    ELLA
          I thought you'd popped to the loo.

                    RUTH
          No, dear. Though now that you mention it.

Ruth hops to her feet, striding around the table and heading
into the hallway.

                    RUTH (CONT'D)
          Don't start without me!

                    ELLA
          I thought—

                    AGGIE
          You really oughta lay off the
          sherry, dear.

MICHAEL, 80s, enters from another doorway. He's grumpy and
thin, swamped by a baggy three-piece suit.

                    AGGIE (CONT'D)
          Did you see the squirrels, dear?

                    MICHAEL
          No. The racket in here must've
          scared em' off. Where's Ruth gone?

                    JACK
          She's popped to the loo. Said we
          should start without her.

                    AGGIE
          She most certainly did not.

                    JACK
          Oh, you know Ruth. She wouldn't want
          us to go hungry. Grub up!

                    ELLA
            Your... funeral.

Ella catches herself repeating the words, frowning as they come out of her mouth.

                    JACK
            At least I won't die with an empty
            stomach.

Jack reaches for the turkey, grabbing a slice and chucking it onto his plate.

Ella turns to Eddie, still plonking away on the piano.

                    ELLA
            Dear, I think we're tucking in.

Eddie doesn't reply, slowly shaking his head. Ella frowns.

                    MICHAEL (O.S.)
            Did you catch the football, Jack?

                    JACK (O.S.)
            Absolute tosh. I could've done a
            better job myself. Should've put me
            in goal.

                    MICHAEL (O.S.)
            I had to switch it off in the end.
            What was the score?

                    JACK (O.S.)
            4-2. 6-5. 7-7. 10-nil-10-nil-10-10-10.

The list of numbers grows incomprehensible, descending into inhuman mumbling. The quiet static returns.

Ella's head snaps around, staring at her dad in horror.

                    ELLA
            What are you saying?

Jack looks to her, shocked at her outburst. He's completely fine.

                    JACK
            Since when have you cared about
            football?

The static stops.

                    ELLA
          I don't... But Eddie's been teaching
          me a bit. Haven't you, dear?

Eddie nods slowly, eyes still fixed to the piano. Ella passes her plate to her dad, letting him serve her some food.

                    ELLA (CONT'D)
          I even scored a goal against him the
          other day. In the park.

                    JACK
          Good sport, Eddie! Glad to hear
          you're keeping her happy.

Jack passes the plate back to Ella, now topped with turkey and veg.

                    ELLA
          He wishes. I'm unstoppable.

She blindly takes a forkful and shoves it in her mouth, recoiling as the food hits her tongue.

She looks down, her Christmas dinner replaced by green peas and fish fingers on a blue plastic plate. The static returns.

                    ELLA (CONT'D)
          What's this?

Ruth strides back into the room. The others freeze with mouths full of turkey, *guilty*.

                    RUTH
          Thanks for waiting.

                    MICHAEL
          Jack said you wouldn't mind.

                    JACK
          I said no such thing.

Ruth breaks into a smile. She tuts, feigning annoyance.

                    RUTH
          So anyway, Ella. How's it going with
          the baby? Is he still being a pain?

                    ELLA
          The baby?

Static. Ella looks to her right, the head of the table
now shared by a high chair, little OLIVER, 0, sitting next
to her.

The static stops.

                    ELLA (CONT'D)
          Oh right! Ollie's doing much better.
          He's started sleeping, and Eddie's
          being *darling* with him.
          I hardly have to get up at all.

                    RUTH
          Sounds like a dream. Your father
          hardly met you until you were four.

                    JACK
          I don't do crying, or faeces. It's
          not my fault.

                    AGGIE
          Can we not talk about *faeces* at the
          dinner table.

Ella laughs, covering her mouth with a hand.

                    MICHAEL
          What *should* we talk about? Dresses?
          Jewellery?

                    AGGIE
          Oh! How're your pearls, dear!

Aggie clasps her hands together, excited. Michael rolls
his eyes.

                    AGGIE (CONT'D)
          Don't you just love them.

                    ELLA
          They're marvellous.

Ella looks down to her pearls. They're still there, but her
dress is gone, replaced by a pair of adidas tracksuit bottoms
and a moth-worn cardigan.

                    ELLA (CONT'D)
            Oh...

Ella looks up to her family. They've *vanished*, the chairs
tipped over and abandoned, the candles blown out. It's dark.

The dining table is a mess, food, plates and cutlery chucked
everywhere. A modern TV set sits at the end, blaring static.

                    ELLA (CONT'D)
            Mummy? Daddy?

She looks across to Eddie. He still sits at the piano with
his head bowed down, hands resting on his lap.

                    ELLA (CONT'D)
            Eddie, dear. What's going on?

She gets out of her chair, walking to her husband.
She reaches out to touch his shoulder...

Eddie slams his hands down on the keyboard, bursting back
into *Deck the Halls*.

                    AGGIE (O.S.)
            These carrots are marvellous,
            darling!

Ella spins around. The dining room is back to normal,
the rest of the family tucking into their dinner.

                    ELLA
            Oh, um... thank you, Granny. They
            almost burnt the house down.

Ella returns to her seat. She looks down at her plate,
the white china and Christmas dinner back in front of her.

She grabs a forkful of turkey, carefully raising it to
her lips. She chews. *Delicious*.

A TALL MAN, 60s, bursts into the room from the hallway,
the TV static roaring as he enters. He's dressed in a modern
black suit, shirt untucked and tie pulled loose.

                    TALL MAN
            It's time for bed.

Ella spins in her chair, face full of horror.

                    ELLA
          Who are you?!

                    TALL MAN
          Come on. Dinner time's over.

He tries to take Ella's food from the table, Ella grabbing
the plate and bringing it to her body, protecting it.

                    ELLA
          Who are you? Dad help!

She turns to her family, but none of them is paying
attention, still eating their meals.

                    ELLA (CONT'D)
          Dad? Mummy?

                    TALL MAN
          Come on.

                    ELLA
          Get away from me! Who are you?
          Get away!

Ella jumps to her feet, shoving the tall man away and turning
to Eddie. The dining room window bursts open, curtains
whipping in the wind. The family doesn't notice.

                    ELLA (CONT'D)
          Eddie?

Eddie continues to play the piano.

                    ELLA (CONT'D)
          Why won't you look at me?

Ella grabs Eddie by the shoulder and spins him around.
His face is blank, smooth skin stretched over his skull.

Ella WAILS, shoving Eddie back and falling into the arms
of the tall man.

The tall man wraps her up, bringing Ella to his chest and
whispering into her ear.

                    TALL MAN
          It's OK. You're safe, I'm here.

Ella starts to sob. She stares at Eddie, where his face should be.

                    ELLA
          Oh Eddie, I can't find your face.
          I can't find your face.

Eddie slowly shakes his head, sombre.

                    TALL MAN
          It's all right, Mum.

                    ELLA
          What?

She tears her eyes away from Eddie, looking up at the tall man.

                    TALL MAN
          It's all right, Mum. I'm here.

4   INT. CARE HOME BEDROOM - NIGHT

The scene behind the tall man shifts, moving from Ella's grand dining hall to a dingy care home bedroom.

It's dark, the room solely lit by a modern TV in the centre of the room. It's playing static.

The Tall Man, (an older OLLIE, 60s) and an older ELLA, 80s, stand in each other's arms.

Ella is now dressed in tracksuit bottoms and a moth-worn cardigan, a faded pearl necklace wrapped around her neck.

                    OLLIE
          It's me, Mum. Ollie.

Ella looks at Ollie through her tears. She furrows her brow, straining to remember. Ollie looks down, hopeful.

Ella slowly shakes her head, eyes glazing over.

                    OLDER ELLA
          Oh bugger.

Ollie sighs. He carefully shifts Ella to the side, gently setting her down in a thick cushioned armchair.

Ella turns, gazing out of the window.

> OLDER ELLA (CONT'D)
> He wishes... I'm unstoppable.

> OLLIE
> I um... I got you a present.

Ollie reaches into his jacket pocket, pulling out a small framed photo.

> OLLIE (CONT'D)
> I found it in the attic.

> OLDER ELLA
> Ollie's doing much better. He's started sleeping, and Eddie's being *darling*...

Ollie leans over his mum, carefully placing the framed photo on her lap. Ella glances down, staring at the image.

> OLDER ELLA (CONT'D)
> Eddie?

She carefully picks up the photo, unsure. She raises it to her face, holding it at eye level.

It shows a young man in a familiar tweed suit. It's Eddie, beaming at the camera.

A smile creeps onto Ella's face, eyes lighting up.

> OLDER ELLA (CONT'D)
> Oh, Eddie.

Ollie smiles, satisfied. He strokes his mum's shoulder.

> OLLIE
> Merry Christmas, Mum.

Ollie walks to the TV set, reaching down and turning it off, the static fizzling out.

Ella doesn't notice, still staring at her husband.

> OLDER ELLA
> Merry Christmas, my love.

Snow falls outside.

<u>THE END</u>

PUTRI KEMUNING

(Extract from play)

Written by

Jennifer Collard

Having recently graduated from the University of East Anglia with a Bachelor of Arts (Hons), Jennifer Collard has diverse experience in acting, costume design and choreography. Most recently, she was appointed as the costume designer for Timberlake Wertenbaker's *The Love of a Nightingale*. Additionally, she has over 10 years of trained dance experience.

jennifercllrd@gmail.com

Translations

Emangiyun: Does not have a literal translation but is a word sung to a baby when trying to put them to sleep. Can roughly mean "sleep, dear baby"

Sayang: Term of endearment

Ayah: Father

Ibu: Mother

Kampung: Village

Ustad Word used in Muslim countries and languages appointed to a teacher or guru

Cirebon, Indonesia. Kemuning is having a crisis as she and her husband, Pratam, prepare for their fifteen-year-old daughter's wedding to a man twice her age. She is bombarded with feelings of uncertainty, knowing the life her daughter will live as a child bride just as she once was. While submerged in these feelings, she is visited by a curious character dressed in a beautiful Javanese wedding dress, the Girl. Realising she has been greeted by her younger self, they both go on a journey to help Kemuning decide whether she should go forward with her daughter's wedding.

SCENE 4

Kemuning and the **Girl** are sitting on the floor facing each other. Beside **Kemuning** there is a bowl of water; she dips a small towel in the water and begins to wipe off the traditional make-up on the **Girl**.

GIRL	It's cold.
KEMUNING	Cold water is good for you, so stop complaining.
GIRL	You sound like Ibu right now.
KEMUNING	I guess so. She used to tell us that the cold water would rejuvenate ourselves and replenish our skin.
GIRL	Yeah.
KEMUNING	So, stop complaining, Ibu knows best.

GIRL   She was such a gentle woman. Sometimes I would want to protect her from the world, not the other way around.

KEMUNING   Yeah, I know what you mean. She was so good to us despite everything.

GIRL   She could've fought for us...

KEMUNING   She was afraid...

GIRL   Yeah? Well so was I.

KEMUNING   I know you were.

GIRL   So? What now? Are you doing to stay afraid like she did?

KEMUNING   I don't want to, but I can't help it. Pratam, he's...he is so despicable. He's almost exactly like Ayah.

GIRL   That's scary.

KEMUNING   You're telling me? I'm married to the man!

GIRL   Ibu must've had it bad then.

KEMUNING   If he could say things he said and do the things he did to his children... imagine what he did to her, his own wife.

Beat.

GIRL   I miss her.

KEMUNING   So do I. Do you think she would be disappointed in us?

GIRL   In me? No.

           In you? Maybe.

KEMUNING   Yeah, I thought so.

GIRL   Do you think she married Ayah out of love?

KEMUNING   Does anyone marry out of love where we come from?

GIRL   I guess not, I wish we did.

KEMUNING   Like in those Barbie movies?

GIRL   Exactly!

Kemuning finishes wiping off the last bit of black paint on the Girl's forehead. The Girl turns around to let Kemuning take out the hair accessories.

	I love those movies!
KEMUNING	I still do.
GIRL	Which one did we watch over and over again?
KEMUNING	Barbie...
GIRL	Barbie as Rapunzel!
KEMUNING	YES!
GIRL	That movie is so good.
KEMUNING	A bit ironic though, don't you think?
GIRL	In what way?
KEMUNING	A beautiful girl trapped in her awful life that she can't escape? She's forced to do the same things every day, her whole life dictated by an evil witch.
GIRL	Except that evil witch is Ayah.
KEMUNING	Suits him doesn't it...

They laugh.

	Shame there isn't a prince that can sweep us away from this life.
GIRL	Those men don't exist anyway.
KEMUNING	Yeah, not here. Those movies become even more unrealistic as I watch them more and more.
GIRL	Well, they're not supposed to be realistic. It's a children's movie.
KEMUNING	But what does it really tell little girls? That we can find our prince and fall in love within a day, then marry the next?
GIRL	Better than your parents finding a man twice your age and marrying you in a week, then you don't even meet him until the day of the wedding.

36.

KEMUNING   That's what I'm saying! They build up this hope within us, just to have it shatter for girls like us.

GIRL   Girls like us?

KEMUNING   You know what I mean.

Beat.

GIRL   We don't need them anyway, right?

KEMUNING   Exactly, what do they have that we need?

GIRL   Money?

KEMUNING   We can make money.

GIRL   We could if we didn't get taken out of school.

KEMUNING   But who did that? Ayah. He was the one who took us out of school and told us that we don't need it.

GIRL   And what is he?

KEMUNING   A man!

GIRL   Yeah, to hell with men!

KEMUNING   Fuck them!

GIRL   What have men done for us anyway?

KEMUNING   They just treat us like reproductive machines, and even then, they only want us to pop out boys.

GIRL   Women are the best.

Kemuning *finishes taking the flowers and jewellery out and begins to braid her hair.*

KEMUNING   We're beautiful, smart, strong.

GIRL   Maybe the men are the ones that should be educated, not us.

KEMUNING   In a perfect world, they would be.

GIRL   We can only pray too.

KEMUNING   You have to stop doing that.

GIRL   Praying?

KEMUNING   Yeah, in what world do I deserve to be treated like this? I've lost all

	hope. I wish this wasn't the case, but I just see myself in every woman walking along the street. Why would God allow this to happen?
	I've even started to sing Ibu's lullaby to put me to sleep every night, not the word of God.
GIRL	Emangiyun?
KEMUNING	Yeah.
GIRL	How did Pratam take it?
KEMUNING	He doesn't know. When he prays, I follow but it doesn't mean anything to me. I don't feel strong enough to continue.
GIRL	That's a shame.

They sing the lullaby.

BOTH:	Emangiyun,
	Emangiyuun,
	Emangiyun,
	Emangiyuun...

Kemuning looks for a change of clothes for the Girl. Meanwhile the girl begins to strip down to her underwear. Kemuning gives the Girl the change of clothes and helps her dress herself again.

They continue to hum the melody of the lullaby while putting the clothes on. Finally, the Girl is dressed in a baggy top and a long batik skirt.

KEMUNING	You look nice.
GIRL	I feel a lot more comfortable without all that on me.
KEMUNING	You even look a little happier.
GIRL	I should not have been in those clothes in the first place.
KEMUNING	I have to say, you did look beautiful.
GIRL	You said that already.
KEMUNING	It's true.
	Come here.

Kemuning sits on the mattress, the Girl comes to sit on her lap. Kemuning cradles her like a baby.

GIRL Will you do better for her?

KEMUNING I can try.

GIRL That's not good enough, Kemuning.

KEMUNING It's all I can promise at the moment.

They stay in that position singing the lullaby softly once again.

BOTH: Emangiyun,

    Emangiyuun,

    Emangiyun,

    Emangiyuun...

SCENE 5

Pratam sits in the living room. Leg shaking, hands clasped together and furrowed eyebrows.

The living room is modest. A beat up couch and one wooden chair. The box TV perched on a small table, he goes to turn it on and sits back down. After a second his stiff posture relaxes.

The Ustad walks in.

USTAD Sitting and watching TV? Do you not have anything to do? The wedding will be here and nothing is done.

Pratam rushes to the Ustad and greets him.

PRATAM Forgive me, Utstad, I just needed a moment to relax; I've been running around all day—

USTAD Where is the child?

PRATAM Sorry?

USTAD Where is your daughter?

PRATAM I'm not sure, I think she might be in her room or out with her friends.

USTAD You don't know where your daughter is? How will I be convinced to go

>   through and officiate this wedding if
>   the man of the house can't keep track
>   of where his child is?

Pratam is silent. Speechless.

>   Do I have to remind you how in demand
>   I am? My time should not be wasted,
>   Pratam.

PRATAM   Yes, Ustad.

Indah walks in.

>   Indah, why isn't there any tea on the
>   table? We have a guest.

INDAH   I'm sorry, sir, I will make that for
                you now.

PRATAM   Also go find my daughter after. The
                Ustad needs to evaluate her. This is
                unacceptable.

INDAH   Yes, sir.

She leaves.

PRATAM   Please, Ustad, stay. There's many
                more things we must agree on before
                the wedding, my daughter is just a
                small part of it.

USTAD   Fine, but this can't happen again,
                Pratam.

PRATAM   I understand.

USTAD   OK, first let's talk about the mosque
                you'll host the initial wedding
                in. I know that you don't have much
                money so you need this wedding to go
                through.

PRATAM   And I take full responsibility.

USTAD   Well, you should. It was your failure
                to support this family that has now
                put them in this position.

Beat.

PRATAM   Y-yes. Right.

USTAD   Stop being so sensitive. No wonder

                    the women live so carefree.
                    They don't know who's in charge.

Indah walks back in with two mugs of tea. She sets them down and leaves.

They both take a sip of the tea and sigh in satisfaction.

PRATAM   If these women didn't know who was in
                    control, would we be presented with
                    such a good cup of tea?

The Ustad chuckles.

USTAD   There is much more than just tea to
                    being a man.

Beat.

                    Look, Pratam, it's never too late
                    to learn. I know you didn't have a
                    strong male figure growing up, but
                    being the man of the family means
                    support.

PRATAM   I know.

USTAD   No, you don't. Being a man means to
                    be strong when everyone else is weak,
                    to be the support when your family
                    is crumbling - that's why you failed.
                    You chose to give up when things got
                    tough.

PRATAM   Losing my firstborn is not anything
                    easy.

USTAD   I never said it was, but it happened.

PRATAM   That boy was supposed to be our
                    ticket to freedom, away from this
                    slum.

USTAD   No, Pratam. You are that ticket to
                    freedom. You can make a better life
                    for your family. You must go through
                    with this wedding so stop playing and
                    sitting around so unsure.

PRATAM   I know, Kemuning keeps telling me
                    it's a bad idea. Honestly, sometimes
                    I believe her.

USTAD   Why?

PRATAM	Because she is young.
USTAD	So was Kemuning, and now look where she is. You have given her a beautiful daughter to love. You must bring honour to your family, Pratam.
PRATAM	But is this the only way? Surely there's more. Is the world really this small?
USTAD	The world is kind and generous if you look the right way.
PRATAM	And this is the right way?

*The **Ustad** nods his head.*

> I understand Ustad.

SCENE 6

***Kemuning** stands in front of the mirror. She assesses her body and begins to run her hands along it. This is the first time in her life that she has ever concentrated so much attention to her temple. Her hands go from her breasts, to her head and her stomach.*

*Enter **Pratam**.*

PRATAM	Oh, you're finally awake. The Ustad is here, we should go meet him together to go over the ceremony tomorrow.
KEMUNING	Actually, Pratam, we need to talk about that.
PRATAM	If you're going to tell me that this is all a mistake, that we shouldn't go through with it, she deserves better...what about us? Don't we deserve better?
KEMUNING	What do you mean?
PRATAM	Don't we deserve to be honoured and respected in the kampung?
KEMUNING	Well, yes.
PRATAM	And how else are we going to do that if we don't go through with this

                    marriage? They are a very respectable
                    family, Kemuning. They will bring us
                    so much fortune and honour.

KEMUNING   I know, but does it have to be now?
                    Why can't we wait a little longer?
                    I don't like this. I don't want her
                    to regret everything in her life, I
                    don't want her to hate us!

PRATAM   She'll be thankful to us.

KEMUNING   No, she won't.

PRATAM   How do you know?

KEMUNING   Because I'm not! I hate this life I
                    live. I have no future. She still has
                    a chance to live the life she wants!

*Silence. Suddenly **Pratam** slaps **Kemuning**.*

PRATAM   Ungrateful bitch. Never speak to me
                    like that again.

*Enter **Indah**.*

INDAH   What's going on?

***Pratam's** eyes never leave **Kemuning**.*

PRATAM   Nothing. Kemuning just got a little
                    emotional again, nothing new.

*He turns to look at **Indah**.*

                    What do you need?

INDAH   The Ustad is asking where the both of
                    you are, then I heard some shouting
                    and got worried.

PRATAM   You have nothing to worry about. I'll
                    go out to entertain the Ustad.

*Turns to look at **Kemuning**.*

                    I'll see you out there in five
                    minutes, yes?

KEMUNING   ...Yes.

***Pratam** leaves.*

INDAH	Are you OK?
KEMUNING	I'm fine. We just had a disagreement, that's all.
INDAH	So, it's all been sorted now?
KEMUNING	Yes.
INDAH	OK well, you better get outside quick.
KEMUNING	Yeah, I'll be there in a minute.

Indah leaves. Kemuning looks in the mirror one last time. She sees herself and just behind her, in the reflection, she sees a Girl dressed in a traditional Javanese wedding outfit.

KEMUNING	You... you look beautiful...

SUPPLY

(Extract from TV script)

Written by

Rosa Cooper-Davies

Rosa Cooper-Davies has worked in the arts since 2008. Starting in youth theatre, she went on to study at Aberystwyth University before beginning a career in participatory arts, which brought her to Norwich where she now studies for an MA in Scriptwriting at UEA. Her passion is to write children's television.

rosa.cooper-davies@live.com

INT. AND EXT. CAR

Paul's mum's red Ford Ka pulls up outside Beechdown Academy with Paul in the passenger seat. It's raining outside and Paul has a coat but no umbrella.

> PAUL
> Thanks for the ride, Mum. See you later.

> PAUL'S MUM
> Make sure you have lunch. Don't let the kids give you a hard time.

She touches his cheek with the palm of her hand.

> PAUL'S MUM
> We're so proud of you, y'know.

Paul rolls his eyes and gives his mum a look.

> PAUL
> I know. I will eat lunch. I won't let the kids give me a hard time. I'll get the bus home. Bye then.

He kisses her on the cheek and gets out of the car. Lifting a briefcase over his head and walking quickly, trying not to run, he heads for the school entrance. It's only now we see that he is wearing a long coat and is actually a teacher, Mr Glebe.

INT. SCHOOL RECEPTION

Mr Glebe (Paul — an utterly nerdy and nervous looking man of around 24, with round glasses, a knitted jumper and a bow tie — think rabbit in headlights, but trying to pretend he's fine)enters through the door. Nobody is sat at the front desk so he sticks his head through the little window.

> MR GLEBE
> Hello? I had a call from—

> RECEPTIONIST
> (not looking away from the screen)
> One moment...

The receptionist types away at the computer without looking at him and apparently not really listening either.

                    MR GLEBE
          It's just— I really—

                    RECEPTIONIST
               (shoving a clipboard towards him)
          Sign in, please.

                    MR GLEBE
          I need to—

                    RECEPTIONIST
          Sign in. If you're late you need to
          sign in on the tardy register and
          then head to your form tutor.

                    MR GLEBE
               (spluttering)
          I'm not— I'm here to— The agency
          sent me!

                    RECEPTIONIST
          Very funny. I know you sixth formers
          think you run the place but—

                    MR GLEBE
          No! I'm a supply teacher!

The receptionist finally looks at him. Not remotely abashed at her mistake.

                    RECEPTIONIST
          Which agency?

                    MR GLEBE
          Tri-Point. Here for the week with
          potential extension?

                    RECEPTIONIST
          I see.

Awkward silence while the receptionist taps away.

                    RECEPTIONIST
          Name?

                    MR GLEBE
          Paul.

                    RECEPTIONIST
              (exaggerated sigh)
         No, NAME. What will the kids be
         calling you? I need to print you a
         pass.

                    MR GLEBE
         Mr Glebe.

                    RECEPTIONIST
         This'll just take a minute.

The receptionist prints a slip of paper and puts it in a
lanyard.

                    RECEPTIONIST
         You're late for morning briefing.

                    MR GLEBE
              (a mix of panic and indignation)
         Morning— what??

                    RECEPTIONIST
         Down the corridor, fourth on the
         right.

The receptionist presses the buzzer and the door to the rest
of the school opens. Mr Glebe runs through.

                    RECEPTIONIST
         And NO RUNNING IN THE CORRIDORS!

Mr Glebe changes pace to be walking awkwardly fast.

CUT TO:

INT. STAFF ROOM — MORNING BRIEFING

The head teacher is already mid flow when Mr Glebe arrives,
addressing the twenty or so teachers gathered in the staff
room, many drinking coffee, some looking at their phones.

                    HEAD TEACHER
         ... and if anyone would like to
         contribute to Adam's whip round or
         sign his get well soon card, or his
         congratulations on the safe birth
         of your triplets—

LIZ
Actually, the shop only had a card for twins.

HEAD TEACHER
OK, we'll just say 'twins plus one'. If anyone wants to sign, speak to Liz.
(noticing Mr Glebe)
And here's Paul who will be covering for Adam this week. Potentially longer.

MR GLEBE
Um... hi, I—

HEAD TEACHER
Unfortunately there's no time for introductions. OK everyone, have a good day. Someone show Paul — Mr Glebe — to Adam's first class please. Everyone else, fetch your form groups from assembly.

The teachers begin to file out — many of them pointedly ignoring Mr Glebe so that they don't have to show him to Mr Driver's classroom. Eventually, it's just him and two others left in there, Mr Islay maths teacher and Miss Betts, biology teacher.

MR ISLAY
Gotta run. Thanks, Karen.

Miss Betts looks at her watch. She does have time.

MISS BETTS
C'mon then — I'll show you to the right room. Got your map?

MR GLEBE
What, these hieroglyphics?

MISS BETTS
(unimpressed)
Yes. Follow me.

INT. SCHOOL CORRIDOR — DAY

Miss Betts walks Mr Glebe along.

              MISS BETTS
So we have no fire drills planned for today, but with Year 8 that's the least of your worries. Their usual teacher Mr Driver has had a bit of a breakdown and what with his wife just having had triplets, the pressure has just been mounting to gargantuan levels — but I'm sure you're robust enough to deal with his class.

Miss Betts looks at Mr Glebe, who drops the map and welcome folder he'd been given on his way in.

              MISS BETTS
Maybe not. Goodbye. And good luck...

Miss Betts opens the door and the sounds of chaos spill out. She steers Mr Glebe into the room and closes the door.

              MISS BETTS
...You're gonna need it.

INT. YEAR 8 CLASSROOM — DAY

Mr Glebe walks into the room and places an overly smart briefcase on the front desk. Chaos reigns and nobody in the class has noticed him.

              MR GLEBE
Excuse me, ladies and gentleman!

No response — the kids continue to throw things at each other, pulling hair and calling names. Nobody in the class could be considered a teacher's pet.

              MR GLEBE
EXCUSE ME!

Pandemonium.

              MR GLEBE
Right!

Mr Glebe unclips his fancy briefcase and pulls out a klaxon, and blasts it for three seconds. The class collectively jump, some of them covering their ears, others yelling in surprise.

>   MR GLEBE
>   (with the air of a sergeant)
>   Right, you horrible lot. I expect
>   respect from you — I'm in charge.
>   Sit your arses down and get out your
>   textbooks!

A child on the front row begins crying. Mr Glebe starts sweating.

CUT TO:

INT. YEAR 8 CLASSROOM

Close up of Mr Glebe's face, still sweating. The chaos is back. This time, he opens the door and clears his throat, trying to get the attention of the class. Nothing. He proceeds to his desk, and slams his briefcase down upon it. Even he seems a little surprised at his assertion.

>   MR GLEBE
>   G-good morning, Year 8.

>   CLASS
>   Good morning, sir.

>   MR GLEBE
>   (turning and writing on the board)
>   My name is Mr Glebe and I'll be
>   taking your class today.

>   KIERAN
>   Sir, what happened to Mr Driver?
>   I can't work if it isn't Mr Driver.

>   MR GLEBE
>   That... um... that's none of your
>   concern.

Lauren, the child who had cried in his imagination, puts up a shaking hand.

>   MR GLEBE
>   Yes, Miss...?

LAUREN
It's Lauren, Lauren Miller.

MR GLEBE
Yes, Lauren?

LAUREN
Is Mr Driver... is he... did he die, sir?

The class erupts.

KIERAN
Mr Driver's dead?/

LAUREN
/Coz I heard that his car was dodgy./

HARRY
/Does that mean I don't have to hand in my homework?/

JOSH
/Sir, why won't you just tell us if Mr Driver is dead?/

MR GLEBE
Settle down now, everyone.

LAUREN
(weeping)
/I can't believe it!/

KIERAN
/Sir, Lauren fancies Mr Driver./

LAUREN
No, I don't!

MR GLEBE
RIGHT!! EVERYONE JUST SHUT THE HELL UP!! I'VE BEEN IN YOUR CLASS LESS THAN FIVE MINUTES. AND THIS IS THE SECOND TIME I'VE HAD TO—

Somebody throws a pencil at him.

MR GLEBE
WHO THREW THAT? WHO THREW THAT??

The class starts laughing.

                    MR GLEBE
RIGHT!

He picks up the overhead projector and hurls it at the children laughing the hardest. The glass shatters and Mr Glebe has a crazed look upon his face.

CUT TO:

INT. YEAR 8 CLASSROOM

The pencil hits Mr Glebe in the shoulder. He takes a deep breath through his nose. He picks up the pencil, and places it on his desk, his jaw clenched.

                    MR GLEBE
    No, Mr Driver is not dead. Now,
    if you could all turn to page 48
    in your textbooks, we'll begin on
    sedimentary rocks.

The class gives a collective groan but does as they are told.

                    MR GLEBE
    Now, who can tell me what a
    sedimentary rock is?

Faharna glances at her textbook and shoots her hand into the air, not waiting to be called on.

                    FAHARNA
    It's made of layers, sir!

                    MR GLEBE
    Yes, well done.

                    HARRY
    So technically, that means an onion
    is a rock too.

                    KIERAN
    Or a cake.

                    JOSH
    What about ogres?

                    MR GLEBE
    Quiet, boys! Cakes and onions

are not rocks. This is NOT a food technology class.

                    FAHARNA
Yeah, idiots. If a cake is gonna be any type of rock, it's gonna be igneous because a cake is made in an oven.

                    KIERAN
CAKE IS AN IGNEOUS ROCK!

                    MR GLEBE
I see your logic there, and technically yes, igneous rocks are produced by a combination of heat and pressure. But alas, a cake is still not a rock because it does not occur naturally.

                    FAHARNA
Even if it's made with organic ingredients, sir? And free range eggs?

                    MR GLEBE
I'm afraid not.

                    JOSH
What about rock cakes, sir?

                    MR GLEBE
Not a rock. Made to look like a rock.

                    HARRY
Marble cake? Sir?

                    MR GLEBE
Also not a rock. The marble in marble cake refers to a process called marbling. It is not a rock.

                    KIERAN
But sir—

                    MR GLEBE
          (with an exaggerated sigh)
Look, I'll prove it to you.

Out of his briefcase comes a chef's toque and a large bowl and wooden spoon.

                MR GLEBE
           (shaking flour directly out of
           his briefcase and into the bowl)
Now, if we imagine that we are making sedimentary rocks here. The raisins, or chocolate chips, or nuts or whatever represent the chemical make up of the rock, which determines what sort of rock it's going to be. So chocolate chips become... say, obsidian, and cherries would be...?

                HARRY
Er... rubies, sir?

                MR GLEBE
Yes, well done!

CUT TO:

INT. YEAR 8 CLASSROOM

                FAHARNA
It's made of layers, sir!

                MR GLEBE
Correct! A house point for you.

                HARRY
Sir, does that mean—

                MR GLEBE
Please raise your hand if you want to ask a question.

Harry raises his hand. Mr Glebe pointedly ignores him and draws a diagram on the board.

                MR GLEBE
As our young learned friend correctly tells us, sedimentary rocks are made of layers. Over millions of years, these build up and are pressed together under

                    their own weight - making rocks.

                         JOSH
                    Rocks are boring, sir.

                         MR GLEBE
                    Are you kidding me? Rocks are
                    AWESOME.

                         JOSH
                    No sir, they're boring.

                         MR GLEBE
                    Oh yeah? How boring is THIS rock?

He opens his briefcase and throws a large sapphire to Josh.

                         MR GLEBE
                    You know that sapphire? It's a rock.
                    And rubies too. Most of the most
                    valuable non-metals are actually
                    rocks.

The class murmur with excitement.

                         JOSH
                    Wow, sir! This has really put me on
                    a new path to become a geologist!
                    What university should I go to?

Mr Glebe beams. A spotlight appears on Mr Glebe, and in front of the whiteboard a banner unfurls saying 'BEST TEACHER EVER' and the class begins to applaud and one of them presents him with a garland and a bottle of champagne which he shakes and sprays over the class as a marching band enters the room playing a dramatic fanfare and confetti begins to fall from the ceiling.

CUT TO:

INT. YEAR 8 CLASSROOM

                         JOSH
                    Rocks are boring, sir.

                    MR GLEBE
               (a look of triumph on his face)
          Not to me, kid. Not to me.

                    JOSH
          Yeah well, I think they're boring.

                    MR GLEBE
          There used to be a saying that only
          boring people get bored.

The class gives a collective 'oooooo!' at this verbal smack
down. Josh turns red.

Camera zooms in slowly on Mr Glebe's face, with a determined
expression. *Eye of the Tiger* starts playing. Short montage of
the rest of class. Mr Glebe takes a whiteboard marker, pulls
the cap off with his teeth, spits it to the side without
looking, and begins drawing a diagram of sedimentary rocks
on the board. Spins the marker in his hand like a cowboy gun.
Straightens his bow tie. Flexes his eyebrows. Kids are in
awe, as it turns out this is actually real, and only the music
was in Mr Glebe's head.

EVERY SEVEN YEARS

(First scene of a stage play)

Written by

Jack Fairey

Jack Fairey is a writer, director, producer, and dramaturg, as well as co-founder of Bedivere Arts Company. His work has been shown at venues in London, Bath, Berkshire, and at the Edinburgh Festival Fringe. Credits include: *Wrath of Achilles* (Ed Fringe 2019) and *The Orator Trilogy* (Radio Drama 2021).

jackfairey@gmail.com

SCENE ONE

POLLY is 14. MARCUS is 14. They are in the back rooms of a Methodist church.

POLLY   You crying?
              S'all right. Don't mind. Keep going.
              Never saw a crying boy before. They
              said you was crying and I was like...
              like, nah.
              Cause boys don't cry, not proper
              cry. Not like sit and sob and red
              eyes and snotty nose and gasping for
              breath cry. When they cry they get
              these real manly tears or like one
              tear that drops down their face all
              dramatic like.
              I've only ever seen boys cry on
              television. Come to think.
              –
              You can stop now if you like. Seen it
              now.
              Or keep going.
              –
              It's fucking cold in here, innit?

MARCUS   Shut the fuck up, Polly.

POLLY   –
              Fucking cold.

MARCUS   It's cause the fire door's open.

POLLY   Right.

MARCUS   Bugger off, Polly.

POLLY   Want me to shut it?

MARCUS   Would you fuck off?

POLLY   I'll shut it.
              –
              There.

MARCUS   Thanks.

POLLY   All right.
              You want me to go now.
              –
              Did you finger Sally Jaggs?
              Cause they're saying you said you
              did but actually you didn't and now
              you're crying and I'm wondering are
              you crying cause you lied or crying
              cause you fingered her and you didn't

	like it. Are you gay? Did you finger Sally Jaggs and find out that vaginas are well scary and decide to be gay and and now you're crying?
MARCUS	I'm not gay. I'm not crying. Fuck, it's cold.
POLLY	Door's shut now. It'll warm up.
MARCUS	It better.
POLLY	So you didn't finger Sally Jaggs?
MARCUS	I did. They just said I didn't.
POLLY	That's why you're crying.
MARCUS	I'm not fucking crying.
POLLY	Right. What was it like?
MARCUS	What?
POLLY	The fingering.
MARCUS	What's wrong with you?
POLLY	Cause I kinda know cause I've done it on me but... — What?
MARCUS	Fuck off, you have.
POLLY	Course I have.
MARCUS	Girls don't... Are you gay?
POLLY	Course girls do.
MARCUS	That's gross.
POLLY	You talk about wanking all the time.
MARCUS	I don't.
POLLY	Not *you* you. Boys.
MARCUS	Don't.
POLLY	Like every third conversation's about dicks.

MARCUS Not every third.
Do girls, seriously?

POLLY   Well yeah.
Not all girls. And they don't talk about it much. But I do. And I can't be the only one.
And I was thinking is it different on someone else when it's someone else's, you know...

MARCUS Muff.

POLLY   Nah, muff's the the hair.
Cootch.

MARCUS Vajajay.

POLLY   Twat.

MARCUS Gash.

POLLY   Urgh gash gash is the fucking worst it's like it's like a wound like an an absence...
—

MARCUS Box.

POLLY   Stop saying the shit ones.

MARCUS What's wrong with box?

POLLY   Makes it sound like a place to put things.

MARCUS Well. It is.

POLLY   Nah, it's not. A box is passive a a a... You know.
It's not passive; stuff doesn't just get put there it like proper...
It's involved.
—
—
Cunt.

MARCUS Fuck off!

POLLY   I know. Shouldn't say it but fuck it.
Cunt.

MARCUS —
Cunt.

POLLY   Cunt! Cunt cunt cunt!

MARCUS Right, that's enough now.

POLLY	Sorry.
MARCUS	We're in a church; don't want God to get mad.
POLLY	Do you believe in him?
MARCUS	No but... Don't believe in ghosts either but I don't say Bloody Mary in front of a mirror, do I?
POLLY	But you will say cunt in a church?
MARCUS	Fuck off! Come sit down. Weird you hovering like that.
POLLY	All right. —
MARCUS	—
POLLY	—
MARCUS	Bit warmer now.
POLLY	Yeah. They opened the fire door.
MARCUS	What?
POLLY	The others. They do it every week. Get here early and open all the fire doors and the back doors and all the doors that are usually locked. Not proper open, just a crack. Means they can get them open from the outside. — Gives them more routes to hide from me. — Don't look like that — you know they do it, you do it too — I've seen you.
MARCUS	Don't. Well, they do. — Sometimes I join in cause they're all doing it but—
POLLY	S'all right, don't mind really. Like a game kind of, isn't it? I'd rather be playing. Like tag or stuck in the mud or something.
MARCUS	Exactly. We're not hiding from you,

	we're hiding... hiding with you. Yeah.
POLLY	Yeah. — Be nice to be one of the ones hiding for a change though just once or twice.
MARCUS	Yeah, definitely. Yeah, I said, I actually said to James, one of us should do it next time.
POLLY	Yeah?
MARCUS	Yeah, but just like you're so good at—
POLLY	At looking.
MARCUS	Yeah, definitely yeah. Like I said, I did say.
POLLY	Thanks.
MARCUS	That's all right.
POLLY	Why'd you finger Sally Jaggs?
MARCUS	Oh cause like... she like... she asked.
POLLY	She asked?
MARCUS	Well, not asked... not like asked asked but... But yeah, asked.
POLLY	Did she like it?
MARCUS	What?
POLLY	Did she like the fingering?
MARCUS	Oh. I don't... I don't know. You're not supposed to really like it, are you? No one really talks about the girl liking it. No one really talks about the guy liking it neither. I guess it's not about liking, it's about doing.
POLLY	Course she's meant to like it.
MARCUS	James says it's like natural selection, isn't it?
POLLY	What is? Fingering?

MARCUS	No, not fingering, but yes yes fingering. All of it. The boy has to chase the girl and the girl gets chased and the fastest boy, the one who catches her gets to... Gets the reward.
POLLY	The girl's meant to like it too.
MARCUS	James says girls who like it are sluts cause they let anyone catch them. Means they don't get the guys with the best genes.
POLLY	You were right.
MARCUS	Yeah? I know. About what?
POLLY	James is an idiot. — Did you like it?
MARCUS	The fingering?
POLLY	The fingering, yeah.
MARCUS	Um yeah. Um. It was all right, yeah all right.
POLLY	So you don't know if she liked it and you thought it was all right? Sounds pointless. You're supposed to like it; I like it when I do it to myself.
MARCUS	Can you not? I get all weird when you talk about that.
POLLY	Sorry. Do you— Nah, never mind. — Do you want to do it to me — on me. Do you want to do it on me?
MARCUS	What? The—
POLLY	Yeah, the fingering.
MARCUS	Why?
POLLY	I don't know. Forget it. I thought maybe you wanted to but—
MARCUS	I do want to.

POLLY   Oh.
          Good.
          You sure?

MARCUS   You sure?

POLLY   Yeah, I'm sure, of course I'm sure.
          So you're not gay?

MARCUS   No.

POLLY   Right, so you want to.
          Now?

MARCUS   Yeah.
          But not *now* now. Like in a minute or two.

POLLY   Sure. So you wanna wait or...?

MARCUS   I don't want to just sit in silence.

POLLY   I wasn't...
          What do you want to do?

MARCUS   Dunno.

POLLY   Why do they hide from me?

MARCUS   I said. For fun.

POLLY   Yeah, but it's always been me, so why me?

MARCUS   Dunno.

POLLY   Fuck off, yeah you do.

MARCUS   Don't.

POLLY   But—

MARCUS   Don't, all right?

POLLY   —
          All right.
          —
          It's just...
          Cause I overheard Jenny and Sakina and they said, they said it was cause I'm too sad.
          Did they mean, like was it sad like crying or sad like uncool?

MARCUS   Dunno, do I? Ask them.
          Sad like crying.
          Both.

POLLY   What's wrong with me being sad?

MARCUS   It's boring.
         Not boring but...
         It's hard. Like hard to know what to
         say to you and stuff.

POLLY   But...
         I don't try to be sad.

MARCUS   Yeah well, we know that. But annoying
         people don't try to be annoying
         and yet they are, aren't they? Some
         people just are things, they can't
         help it, they just are.

POLLY   All right.
         -
         But what's wrong with being sad? You
         haven't said.

MARCUS   Nothing's right, nothing's wrong with
         being sad, all right?

POLLY   Then why—

MARCUS   Because people are shit, Polly, and
         we're shit and we make mistakes and
         people like people who are happy and
         fun and not always fucking crying all
         the time.
         -
         Sorry.
         -
         Polly.
         -
         I didn't mean it.
         -
         Come on.

POLLY   I'm too sad for you. So I'm not gonna
         speak anymore.

MARCUS   You just did.

POLLY   From now.

MARCUS   You did it again. You're shit at
         this.

POLLY   Fuck off, Marcus!

MARCUS   Oh come on, I'm kidding. Come back
         and sit down.
         Polly, you know I'm joking, right?

POLLY   No.

MARCUS   Polly...

POLLY Don't get what you want from me.

MARCUS What?

POLLY Don't fucking get what you want from me, do I?
Fuck sake.
First I'm too sad then when I'm not sad I talk too much. What do you want me to do? Just tell me and I'll do it, I swear.
Just tell me and I'll do it.

MARCUS I don't want you to do anything.

POLLY Yeah.

MARCUS I don't, Polly, I just want you to be you, all right?

POLLY Then why do you hide from me and laugh at me and—

MARCUS I'll stop — I'll make them stop.

POLLY Sure you will.

MARCUS I will, Polly, I will, you'll see. You'll see.
Now will you come and just... just sit?

POLLY You'll make them stop?

MARCUS Yeah.

POLLY You promise?

MARCUS Will you just sit?

POLLY —
Thanks.

MARCUS That's all right.
I like you Polly. All weird and sad as you are. I like you.

POLLY —
Do you...
—
Like, do you still want to...

MARCUS What?
Oh.
Well...
Yeah all right, why not?

POLLY Not why not, like do you actually want—

MARCUS	Course I want to, course I do.
POLLY	OK, awesome.
MARCUS	You want to right?
POLLY	Why? Trying to work out if James would think I'm a slut?
MARCUS	No course not. James is a dick. I... I just want to make sure.
POLLY	I want to. It's just bodies, right? Just skin and flesh and everything underneath. Not like we're touching souls. Like people say, they say that the cells in our body right, you know the cells?
MARCUS	Yeah I know about cells.
POLLY	They say that they like... Regenerate. And people say that the cells regenerate; they die and become new cells. And they do so at a rate that means every seven years you've basically got an entirely new body. No cells remain from the person you were seven years ago. So this and us is just bodies and bodies don't matter cause they're... They're expendable. So yeah. I want to.
MARCUS	Good, yeah. Bodies and cells and stuff. Me too. - Now?
POLLY	Well, yeah. Like my dad's coming in twenty minutes so it's kind of now or never.
MARCUS	All right, all right now. - - How do I... - How do we start?
POLLY	Well, do you want to touch my tits? They're not big but they're all right.

MARCUS	OK. – Now?
POLLY	Yeah, just... Yeah. – Ouch. Ouch. Bloody hell Marcus, you're not trying to juice them.
MARCUS	Sorry.
POLLY	Just a gentle... Yeah. That's better. – Your hands are shaking.
MARCUS	They're not.
POLLY	They are — I can feel them.
MARCUS	Then it's cause it's fucking cold in here.
POLLY	It's not cold anymore. – You can let go now if you... – Marcus?
MARCUS	–
POLLY	Marcus, you all right?
MARCUS	–
POLLY	Are you crying again?
MARCUS	What if I am?
POLLY	Nothing, it's OK, it's really OK. Like we don't have to, you know. We don't have to. It's OK. – Want me to go?
MARCUS	Could you just... And I'm not gay or anything, so don't go telling people, but could you just... Could you just like hug me or something?
POLLY	Like this?
MARCUS	Yeah. Yeah like that.

                        —
                        Thanks.

POLLY   S'all right.
                Do you wanna like talk or...
                Or just this?

MARCUS   Just this.
                Is that—

POLLY   Yeah, yeah sure.
                Just this.

A LOVE LETTER TO ALL THOSE
WHO CARE ABOUT JACK

(A radio play)

Written by

Sebastian Garbacz

Sebastian Garbacz is a Polish-born playwright, director and actor based in Norwich. He wrote and directed several award-winning plays performed in venues across Norwich and beyond, including the Edinburgh Fringe. In 2019, he was awarded the David & Jo Spinks Award for Outstanding Contribution to Drama.

sebastian.garbacz@outlook.com

CRICKETS

A TRAIN MOVING IN THE DISTANCE, SLOWLY GETTING CLOSER

JACK (V.O.) Do you ever think about how fast your thoughts are? It's incredible really. If speaking is like someone walking, then thinking is like a speeding train.

(CLOSE) THE TRAIN MOVES VERY FAST

CUT BACK TO THE TRAIN COMING FROM THE DISTANCE AGAIN

By the time the train gets here, I could probably just about finish saying these last few sentences. Perhaps add a little dramatic pause and say...

...'Goodbye world, you've not been too bad,' before the train flattens my head against the track. But I'm still here... God, thinking is quick...

THE TRAIN IS GRADUALLY GETTING CLOSER

I always wonder what would happen. I mean... would the train derail? It wouldn't, right? Or would it? It can't be that easy to derail a train. If it was, it would happen all the time, wouldn't it? But... like... if it's a whole body and the train goes over it, wouldn't it lift up and...

Oh, what am I talking about... it's a fucking train, it weighs like tons, of course it wouldn't lift up.

THE TRAIN

How is it going to kill me then? Is it just going to push me?

Oh wait, but does it mean what I said before doesn't make any sense? That it would flatten my head against the track... that's a shame. I liked that sentence. Very... visceral. Flatten my head against the track.

Visceral. Is that the word? Vivid? Raw?

Raw is nice. Brutal.

Brutal works. Immediate.

Yes, immediate! Oh that's a great word. So... ahh that's such a great word! Brutal is simpler though. More... direct.

Direct! That's a good word. It is quite direct. The sentence I mean.

...

So will the train just push me? I mean... I don't know if 'push' is an appropriate word, at that speed.

THE TRAIN

Here we go.

HE STARTS CRYING, HE'S PANICKING

God, what am I doing here? I can't do this to them. They don't deserve it. Oh God.

HE TAKES A SUDDEN DEEP, SNOTTY BREATH THROUGH THE NOSE

THEN A LONG SHAKING EXHALE WITH HIS MOUTH, WHICH GETS CALMER TOWARDS THE END

THEN ANOTHER MUCH CALMER INHALE AND EXHALE WITH HIS MOUTH

I'm sorry about all you'll have to go through. But I can't do this anymore. I don't deserve it. Or maybe I do, who knows?

Do I? Do I deserve it?

No, fuck you, I don't! I know I don't! Fuck you!

I don't.

I don't.

I don't.

HE STARTS CRYING AGAIN

I DON'T!

I DON'T.

...

I don't.

HE CALMS DOWN

My skull will definitely shatter.

I wonder what that would look like. For some reason I'm thinking of glass being smashed. But surely a human skull is tougher than glass. Maybe it's like Gorilla Glass. I remember that YouTube video about it. The one with Myth Busters in it. What are their names...

I know the old one is Jamie. Why do I know his name, but not the cool one's? What is his name? God, I can't remember. Not Charlie, not Danny. I bet I'm way off...

Oh God, I'm probably so embarrassingly off. It's probably something like... Richard, or Sebastian? Hang on, doesn't it start with S? S... Sam? Or Simon! Is it Simon? I think it might be.

THE TRAIN

Christ, I'm lying on rail tracks, at half past midnight, waiting for a train to shatter my skull and I'm thinking of fucking Myth Busters.

Not of fucking them, of them. Fucking as an adjective.

What if I do want to fuck them? And it's just my brain telling me that. No! What the fuck! Of course I don't want to fuck them! They're so old.

And I'm not gay.

Not that I wouldn't like to be.
I mean, I wouldn't. I mean...

Oh God, was that homophobic? Am I a homophobe? I don't think I am.

...

Maybe I am gay? Who doesn't sometimes find other men attractive? But I wouldn't want to fuck a man.

...

No! It's not because I think there is something wrong with that, of course there isn't and I never thought there is, I am not a homophobe, it's just because I'm not gay and there is nothing wrong with a straight man not wanting to fuck other men.

God! Why am I explaining myself to my own thoughts?! I am not a homophobe and what I thought wasn't homophobic, full stop.

...

But even if it was homophobic then if I were to say it out loud, I wouldn't, because I don't actually think that. Now full stop.

JACK SIGHS

Why are you doing this to me, eh brain? Why do you do this to yourself?

It's even you who hates yourself for doing that! Why do you hate yourself?!

...

Why do you hate yourself...

...

(NOT V.O.) WHY! THE FUCK! DO YOU! FUCKING! HATE! YOURSELF! SO! FUCKING! MUCH! YOU PATHETIC! LITTLE! BOY!?

**AS HE SAYS THAT THERE'S A REPEATED
THUMPING NOISE AND THE SOUND OF
THE GRAVEL MOVING UNDER HIS BODY
AS HE WRIGGLES, HITTING THE TRACKS
WITH HIS BODY EVERY TIME HE SHOUTS**

(V.O.) Yes, you're a boy! And I don't fucking care how old you are! You're a boy! A pathetic fucking little boy! And nobody loves you! And nobody ever did and nobody ever will! Cause you're a pathetic little fucking cunt! That's what you are!

A pathetic little fucking cunt! Do you undersTAND THAT? A PATHETIC LITTLE FUCKING CUNT!

SILENCE (BUT THE TRAIN)

VERY SUBTLE WEEPING

I guess the train wasn't as close as I thought. Still, it will be here any moment now.

...

Any moment...

**SILENCE. OVER THE FOLLOWING LINES
HE GETS CLOSER AND CLOSER TO PANIC
AND STARTS CRYING**

Is this selfish?

No! Fuck you! Not again!

But is it?

Shut up! No it isn't! I've already been through this so many times! It isn't selfish! It isn't!

But it is. For me it'll be over. Nothing. Nothingness. But it's them who will have to carry all that pain.

But what about my pain?! Isn't that enough of a reason?! Isn't that too much to take?!

Yeah it is. So imagine how much it will be for them to take.

Why do I always have to be the fucking brave one?! Hide the scars and smile, eh?! Eh?!

Why me, eh?!

No, cause I can't let them fucking suffer over me being too fucking weak, eh?!

Fuck you!

FUCK YOU!

> **THE SOUND OF THE GRAVEL AS HE, CRYING HYSTERICALLY, GETS UP**
>
> **THE HUGE OVERWHELMING SOUND OF THE TRAIN SPEEDING PAST**
>
> **IT GOES AWAY**
>
> **WEEPING**

Fuck you. Fuck all of you who care.

> **WEEPING**
>
> **HE CALMS DOWN**
>
> **HE TAKES OUT HIS PHONE, CALLS; THERE'S A SIGNAL**

(NOT V.O.) Hey Mum. Yeah, I know, sorry, it took longer than I thought. Yeah it was nice, Millie says hi. Can you pick me up? Yeah, same place as last time.

LOVE UNDERGROUND

(Extract from play)

Written by

Sam Gillett

Sam Gillett is an actor, writer and sound designer. He completed his BA in Acting at the Guildhall School of Music and Drama in 2015. Film credits include *A Caribbean Dream* (2017), *I'll Find You* (2020) and *Honey Street* (tbc). He is closely affiliated to *Matchstick Theatre Company* and has performed in several plays at their New Cross venue, *Matchstick Piehouse*. Sam was nominated for Best Supporting Actor in the 2018 British National Film Awards. His first play was listed in the 2020 Theatre Royal Haymarket competition, *Pitch Your Play*.

samgillett29@gmail.com

ACT ONE

Late evening. Autumn 2021. Somewhere in Epping Forest. A tattered banner droops between two trees. The message 'Love Underground' graffitied in brilliant colour. Chinese lanterns hang from branches and an enormous eye painted onto plywood is stapled to a trunk. A rickety sound system is stacked upstage. Nearby, two turntables, a mixer, and a microphone positioned on a makeshift pallet desk. Floodlights are fixed to the surrounding trees. A cable connects the lights and sound system to a petrol generator. Lying around on the dirt — portable crates of techno records, a trestle table, ice buckets, packets of ice, bottles of water and squash, and various decorative flourishes — tinsel jellyfish, mannequins dressed in flamboyant 90s tracksuits.

Bosco, forties, muddles into view, fairy lights lassoed around his arm. He sets about arranging them. Johnny Rambler, late twenties, follows in a tangle of black leads. Solemnly wire matches between turntables and sound system. Digby Ives, early twenties, trails behind, struggling under the weight of several packs of beer. Deposits them next to the trestle table and starts assembling a bar. The three can continue to busy themselves prepping in various ways, unless stated otherwise, for the entire first act.

JOHNNY	Should not have munched that acid. Feels like I got haemorrhoids in my throat and a headache up my arse.
BOSCO	Digby, your acid is wretched.
DIGBY	It's Swiss needlepoint.
JOHNNY	Swiss needlepoint?
BOSCO	He just says words, don't he?
JOHNNY	Tasted like murder, mate. Tongue's still numb as fuck.
BOSCO	Same.
JOHNNY	Spiced with some research chemical must be.
DIGBY	John, with all due respect, you wouldn't know quality if it had its cock in your ear.
BOSCO	He's flirting with you again.

JOHNNY	I know. He always gets like this when he's lit.
BOSCO	How d'you know quality's got a cock anyway? Sexist.
JOHNNY	*Swiss needlepoint.*
DIGBY	It's the choicest acid you've ever eaten. Shut up and enjoy.

Pause. The three continue their work diligently.

BOSCO	Oi, quality has definitely got a vaj.
JOHNNY	It's got both I reckon, so it can give itself a stab whenever.
BOSCO	That would be quality.
DIGBY	Did Andy say who was warming up?

Pause

JOHNNY	Dunno.... Bosco'll warm up.
BOSCO	I ain't really got nothing to warm up with. Just a tonne of filthy stinking bangers afraid.
DIGBY	What about you, John?
JOHNNY	Ain't brought nothing calm neither to be fair.
BOSCO	Suppose we could pitch down a banger to a more temperate BPM.
JOHNNY	Nah, a pitched down banger don't sound right. Only sound like a pitched down banger.
BOSCO	Mmmm wise words.
DIGBY	Just 'cus... I've been sitting on a bit of downtempo stuff and I thought... maybe I could try play it out...

Johnny and Bosco pause to consider.

BOSCO	Oh.
JOHNNY	Can't spin though can you, mate?
DIGBY	Well. I thought I'd give it a go.
BOSCO	Give it a go? It's a hard-earned craft.

JOHNNY   Can't just give it a go.

DIGBY   Yeah, right. How'd *you* start then?

BOSCO   Years of practice. And then, *maybe* then, you're decent enough to play out. Plenty of dudes who'll dedicate themselves. Splash four grand on the decks and whatever. High hopes that one day they can call themselves a top selector. But talent. That's a rare thing. You either got it or you ain't. And all that money and all them hours spent alone hunched over your technics learning to beat match... *what was it all for*? For fuck all perhaps. For fuck all at all.

JOHNNY   Many a deck broke a man's spirit. Believe.

DIGBY   I can mix.

Pause

I've been practising.

JOHNNY   Oh. He's been practising.

Pause

BOSCO   Have you asked Andy?

DIGBY   Nah.

Pause

BOSCO   Thing is Digby, if you turn out to flop.

JOHNNY   Turn off the punters.

DIGBY   I won't.

Pause. Johnny has finished wire matching. Now sets about hanging a projector screen between branches.

JOHNNY   Tell you what. Rig's set up. Show us how it's done.

BOSCO   Ooof. Cruel.

Digby fetches a record crate, smaller than the others, and places it beside the turntable. Searches for a record.

DIGBY   Think I can't do it?

JOHNNY   I wondered whose that was. Adorable.

DIGBY   Piss off.

BOSCO   What's he gonna open with? The crowds chew their fingernails.

Digby fishes out a record.

DIGBY   Picked this one up in Croydon and uh... yeah... rocks pretty hard.

JOHNNY   We'll be the judge of that.

Digby, Johnny and Bosco share smirks. A stillness. Johnny and Bosco stop prepping. Digby delicately places a record on the mat, lowers needle onto wax and presses play. We hear Ravel's 'Pavane Pour Une Infante Defunte' melancholically swirl, although that's not what Digby's playing. He's playing 'Pillock' by The Mashupheadz pitched down, as awe-inspiring to their ears.

BOSCO   UK flavours.

JOHNNY   A solid opener.

BOSCO   Sounds like 1998 to me.

Digby adjusts the equalisation. Begins to search for another record. The three spend a time attentively listening. Gradually begin to return to their jobs.

BOSCO   Pretty delish actually. Robust bit of tech-house.

JOHNNY   Unique vocal sample.

BOSCO   Undeniably tech-house but you're right, Johnny... unique within the tech-house genre.

Another pause. Johnny and Bosco listen closely. Digby is now fixatedly attempting to beat match a new record.

JOHNNY   Just a hint of broken beat.

BOSCO   Undertones. Undertones of broken beat. Definitely.

Another pause. A new passage of Ravel gets Johnny and Bosco very excited. Pillock by the Mashupheadz has evidently dropped.

BOSCO	Fuck me tenderly!
JOHNNY	Filth! Pure filth!
BOSCO	Spectacular use of a 303.
JOHNNY	You've pitched down a banger!

Another pause.

BOSCO	Oi, let's have an ID.
DIGBY	Dig it yourself, mate.
BOSCO	Coy fucker.

Another pause. Johnny and Bosco are trying to name it.

JOHNNY	Oi, is it the Poon Tang Clan?
DIGBY	Nah.
BOSCO	Is it The Delinquents?
DIGBY	Nah.
JOHNNY	Is it Bushwacka?
DIGBY	Close.

Andy Jo, fifties, enters in novelty sunglasses and a pink wig, wheeling a trolley full of crisps, soft drinks, and nitrous oxide tanks. Digby pauses the record, ashamed to be caught not working. Ravel warps to a halt. Digby busies himself as do Johnny and Bosco.

ANDY	Tech House Phenomena Part Two. Eukahouse. Pure Science A-side. Matt Benjamin and Nate Coles of Bushwacka B-side.
JOHNNY	Nah — mate it weren't.

Andy raises a finger to silence Johnny.

ANDY	Under the guise of their side project...

Pause

ANDY	The Mashupheadz.

Johnny and Bosco look to Digby for confirmation.

DIGBY	Done it one.

JOHNNY   Bastard. What's the tune called?

ANDY   The tune's called what John here's are a fine example of...

JOHNNY   Oh yeah?

DIGBY   (*giggling*). Tunes called 'Pillock'.

ANDY   I was pals with The Mashupheadz.

DIGBY   Really?

Andy tosses cartons of Rubicon Lychee to the three.

ANDY   Yeah. Me and The Mashupheadz go way back.

DIGBY   So sick... Must have got up to all sorts, what?

ANDY   Oh yeah. All sorts. Exactly. Once we played back to back for Prince Charles.

JOHNNY   No, you didn't.

ANDY   We did. It's the truth. Used to be an avid tech-house fan, Prince Charles. Yeah. And let me tell you, they don't call him Charlie for nothing.

JOHNNY   Fuckin' joker, Andy.

ANDY   I wish I were joking. Close to a week that birthday party lasted. Would have gone on if I hadn't nearly died. See, Charles had arranged a crew of medics with saline drips in one of the throne rooms. Yeah. Soon as the comedown got too rough you could pay them a visit. Whacked a catheter in your arm and drained out the toxins. Jack you up venison testosterone too if you were hardcore. Too much for me personally. Them Windsors were up for days. An education no doubt. Taught me the true meaning of a royal bender.

DIGBY   How'd you nearly die?

ANDY   Well look. The Mashupheadz, they're lovely blokes. But they always struggled to keep their flies done up. Fundamentally kind-hearted individuals but would gladly fuck a

                    goat if it came to it. Bit like you,
                    Johnny...

JOHNNY   Oh, fuck off.

ANDY   Camilla Parker Bowles is racking
                    fatty lines on the mantelpiece.
                    She's been up for six days and her
                    tongue's gone blue. Nathan from The
                    Mashupheadz, he says to Camilla,
                    sweetheart, let me suggest something.
                    You're in dire need of hydration. Got
                    some Lucozade Sport stowed in the
                    paddocks if care to come with. He's
                    a charming dude is Nate, so Camilla
                    obliges. Takes a stroll with him
                    to the paddocks. One thing comes to
                    another, and soon the whole party is
                    looking out the window, watching as
                    the pair go at it, top of a horse.

JOHNNY   Top of a horse?

ANDY   That's right. Doing laps around the
                    paddock. Riding a horse and riding
                    each other. Now Prince Charles
                    weren't thrilled about this. No.
                    Not one bit. I'd *recommended* The
                    Mashupheadz. *He'd* wanted The Chemical
                    Brothers, but they were off on tour.
                    I said to him, look Charlie, darling,
                    I know couple of dudes dick hard on
                    the Chemical Brothers.

DIGBY   Absolutely.

ANDY   He said tremendous. Let's have 'em.
                    But now this horsey business is going
                    on out the window, and it's firmly on
                    me, see? I'm to blame.

DIGBY   So, what did he do? Prince Charles.

ANDY   Well, this was thirty years ago.
                    Charles was stronger then. Plus,
                    he was charging on that aforesaid
                    mentioned venison testosterone. He
                    comes over to me. Grabs me by my
                    necklace. Starts to spin me round
                    like he's throwing the hammer.
                    Releases the necklace and I smash
                    through a window, drop two storeys,
                    think it's all over but then a posse
                    of ten corgies cushion my fall.

JOHNNY   Oi Andy, Digby's asking if he can warm up.

ANDY   Oh yeah?

JOHNNY   We was just getting him to mix a few tunes.

ANDY   Can you mix, Digby?

DIGBY   Yeah, I can.

ANDY   How long you been at it?

DIGBY   Couple of months.

ANDY   Let's see your hands.

DIGBY   Reading my palms.

ANDY   Checking for blisters.

DIGBY   Oh.

ANDY   You haven't got any.

DIGBY   Nah...

ANDY   Would if you'd been practising.

DIGBY   I have been practising.

ANDY   Not hard enough. Clearly. Been initiated?

DIGBY   What?

ANDY   Did the boys perform the ritual?

DIGBY   Nah...

ANDY   Tell him, Johnny.

JOHNNY   Oh um... it's tradition to... before you first play you gotta... prick your arm with a technic needle.

DIGBY   Piss off.

ANDY   It's the way it's always been.

DIGBY   Like fuck it has.

BOSCO   Digby, how many dudes would offer their right bollock just to—

JOHNNY   Just to have the *chance*.

BOSCO   Dreaming night and day of it.

DIGBY   Yeah, and so am I... think about it all the time... Playing tunes and that.

ANDY   Oh yeah?

DIGBY	Yeah. Absolutely.

Pause

ANDY	Roll up your sleeves then.

Andy eyes Digby with earnest intensity. Digby caves, rolls up one of his sleeves slowly.

You'll wanna lie down for this.

Digby affected by a sudden solemnity, agrees to lie down.

Johnny, grab a needle.

Johnny does so. Hands it to Andy who begins to knight Digby with it. Tapping his head, heart and shoulders. Head tipped skyward, he proceeds with the ritual.

Oh, mighty selector. Crate digger celestial. Oh, spinner in the sky. In the name of techno, acid and hardcore... of garage, speed garage and grime... of jungle, drum and bass, breakbeat and *trance*—

DIGBY	Fucking hurry up with it.

ANDY	Of *trance*... progressive house... tech-house... ambient house... funky house... minimal house... deep house... electro house... Never met you sir please get out of my house.

DIGBY	Fuck this.

ANDY	We hereby ask that you bless this... right dishonourable gentleman, as he embarks upon his debut with the wickedest of all parties ever to do it.

Wolf whistles and whoops from Johnny and Digby.

Oh heavenly MC. Oh master of all ceremonies. Imbue this mortal fuckwit with your divine powers of selection, your supreme knack for beatmatching, and your never diminishing party stamina. Guide him through the treachery of comedowns, sweeten them sour acid trips and please please

please help him out of K-holes. Most
crucially... protect him at all times
from the dark forces that prey on
his exploits, that he may rotate,
for hours on end, unperturbed by the
po-po and annoying drunk cunts... And
now... so that you may know of his
essence, we will perform the age-old
rite... Digby.

Digby, wincing, lends his forearm.

ANGELFISH

(Short Film)

Written by

Katey Hoffman

Katey Hoffman is a Canadian scriptwriter based in the UK. As a playwright, her award-winning work continues to tour North America. Katey is also co-creator of *LXDY PARTS*, a popular feminist sketch comedy show showcasing some of Canada's funniest female-identified performers. In 2018, *Saint Joan's Seven*, an original screenplay co-written by Katey, was selected as one of six scripts to compete in the Toronto International Film Festival's Pitch This! competition. She's currently working on an original screenplay commission with Telefilm Canada and writing a new play for Green Thumb Theatre set to premiere in their 2021/2022 season.

CLOSE-UP on a fish tank.

A radio softly plays 'If It Makes You Happy' by Sheryl Crow underneath the colourful guppies and goldfish swimming amongst the fake coral.

Their mouths open and close, bubbles float to the surface. It's supposed to be peaceful.

After a moment, a brave angelfish with huge eyes and kissy-lips approaches the glass. It's cute for a fish.

It stares at us as if to say, 'HELP ME.'

A hand gently taps the glass.

OFFSCREEN a woman clears her throat.

INT. CLINIC — WAITING ROOM — DAY — 2001

The throat-clearer is a stern RECEPTIONIST (50s) sitting at a desk behind a glass partition.

She points to a sign near the tank reading:

DO NOT TAP THE GLASS! THIS HAS BEEN PROVEN TO TRAUMATIZE THE FISH!

ANDREA (17), the glass-tapper, clad in an oversized plaid shirt and a fringe she's obviously cut herself, rolls her eyes. She has a clipboard on her lap.

She pulls out one of those Nokia cell phones shaped like a small brick.

ON SCREEN a text reads: 'exam in 5 mins where the fuck r u???'

She starts to respond but deletes it. She puts her phone away.

She turns her attention to the clipboard and finishes signing a paper, pocketing the fancy pen inscribed with the clinic's flowery logo.

She crosses the room, handing the clipboard to the receptionist who shoots her a steely side-eye before going back to her late-90s computer.

Andrea sits down next to the fish tank again. Bored, she takes in the room.

Uncomfortable pastel pink chairs, a smattering of teen magazines on a coffee table, an inspirational poster of a cute kitten hanging from a clothesline reading:

HANG IN THERE!

A YOUNG WOMAN softly cries in the corner, leaning against a helpless YOUNG MAN.

Across from her, another YOUNGER WOMAN chews her bright-green nails.

At her feet lie several bright-green half-moon discards.

Andrea leans over to grab a magazine, idly opening it to a random page.

INSERT: a quiz titled, 'IS YOUR CRUSH BOYFRIEND MATERIAL?' Someone has already filled it out. The answer is circled: 'HE'S GOT SOME GROWING UP TO DO!'

Andrea tosses the magazine back on the coffee table.

A WELL-DRESSED WOMAN (late 30s) in business casual enters the clinic.

She checks in with the receptionist.

                       WOMAN
                  (inaudible)
          Hi... Peterson? ... Right... OK.
          Thank you.

The secretary hands her a clipboard.

She sits in an empty seat near to Andrea. Andrea can't help but stare at her – she really doesn't seem to fit in here.

The Well-Dressed Woman looks at the clipboard, a bit stunned. At a loss.

After a moment, Andrea digs in her pocket. She hands her the stolen pen.

Well-Dressed gives her a grateful nod. A pen. That's what she needed. She gets to work signing the form.

Andrea pulls out her cell again, takes a look, and puts it away.

A woozy-looking YOUNG WOMAN comes through the other door, with leads further into the clinic, led by a solemn MOTHER.

Andrea watches them as they make their way to the exit incredibly slowly.

She looks back to the fish tank beside her.

The angelfish from previous floats on the surface, belly-up.

Andrea's mouth falls.

                    NURSE (O.S.)
          Andrea Bernard?

PRELAP: The steady BEEP of a heart monitor.

INT. CLINIC — LATER

POV: Andrea. A ceiling painted to look like a blue sky with fluffy white clouds. It's supposed to be calming.

REVERSE: CLOSE ON Andrea who lies on an operating table, staring at the sky-ceiling.

A series of QUICK CUTS:
- The NURSE arranges NARROW FORCEPS on a trolley.
- The DOCTOR gloves up.
- A gloved ANAESTHESIOLOGIST wipes the back of Andrea's hand with an alcohol swab.

                    ANAESTHESIOLOGIST
          Sharp scratch now.

Using a needle, he inserts a cannula on his patient.

Andrea inhales sharply.

POV: Andrea again. The 'calming' clouds. But after a moment, they begin to move. Slowly at first and then quickly gaining speed.

The clouds begin to swirl and make shapes.

A beating heart.

A cock and balls.

A speeding car.

An angelfish.

A middle finger.

DARKNESS.

INT. HIGH SCHOOL — HALLWAY — DAY

A locker-lined hallway with freshly waxed floors. Empty, eerie, illuminated by aggressive fluorescent lights.

A distorted version of 'If It Makes You Happy' plays over the school intercom. We still hear the faint BEEPs of the heart monitor.

POV: Andrea as we walk. The hallway looks like it could go on forever.

We hear voices but we can barely make out what they say. It's as if they're underwater. Or maybe we are.

                    NURSE
               (inaudible)
        Last night... That new Mexican
        place... Thirty-second and...

We walk further.

                    DOCTOR
        Sounds nice... What does he... Lower...
        That's good...

Passing empty classrooms.

                    NURSE
        Engineer for...

                    DOCTOR
        Ooooh. So do you think... Right
        there... Good...

We approach a closed door. Our hand – Andrea's hand – reaches out to turn the handle.

                    NURSE
          Maybe... Do you need...

                    DOCTOR
          ... Thank you.

We open it.

The desks are full of STUDENTS writing an exam. A frowning TEACHER sits at the front.

Their heads all turn slowly and simultaneously to stare at us as if to say, 'where the fuck were u???'

REVERSE: Andrea opens her mouth to explain, but a flood of water spills out of her mouth like a trickling faucet.

She begins to choke violently - something is stuck in her throat - no one moves to help her. She hacks in vain, her face growing purple. In desperation, she resorts to punching herself in the stomach repeatedly.

Finally an angelfish flies out of her mouth and hits the grumpy teacher on the forehead.

Everyone in the class screams.

EXT. CLINIC — LATER

Andrea, looking like hell, leans against the building, smoking a cigarette.

She lets her head fall back against the decaying stucco.

POV: Andrea. The sky is dull and grey. No clouds.

                    VOICE (O.S.)
          Murderer!

Andrea looks over at the lone protester: a snarling ELDERLY WOMAN wearing a sandwich board with a crude drawing of a foetus on it.

A tense beat as she and Andrea lock eyes.

WE ZOOM IN on their widened eyes. Back and forth. A staring contest.

A suspenseful beat – who will blink first?

The Elderly Woman does.

The corners of Andrea's mouth twitch upwards.

The receptionist pops her head out and angrily points to a sign that reads:

NO SMOKING!

EXT. 7-11 CONVENIENCE STORE – 1990 VOLKSWAGEN JETTA – LATER

Andrea sleeps, mouth open, in the passenger seat.

A hand taps on the window.

She wakes with a start and unrolls it.

The hand offers her a huge plastic Big Gulp cup.

INT. 1990 VOLKSWAGEN JETTA – MOVING – LATER

OWEN (17), baby-faced and lanky in a shabby denim jacket, drives.

Andrea sits next to him, sipping her Big Gulp.

He steals glances at her, not knowing what to say.

He turns on the radio – it's that 2001 hit 'I'm A Survivor' by Destiny's Child. The chorus plays for three seconds before Andrea turns it off.

Silence.

She reclines the passenger's seat as low as it will go.

POV: Andrea. The ceiling of the car is worn and blemished with water stains. We stay on the ceiling as we drive.

>   OWEN (O.S.)
>   I'm sure she'll let you do a make-up
>   test.
>   ...
>   Probably.

END

EVENING WALK

(Extract from play)

Written by

Mehmet Izbudak

In a previous incarnation, Mehmet Izbudak has worked as assistant director at Scottish Opera and directed a summer season of plays with Christchurch Repertory Company. Writing credits include *Dr and Mrs Faustus*, a contemporary marketing slant on the legend, and *Demons*, an adaptation of Dostoevsky's novel at the Studio Theatre, Wimbledon in 2003 and 2012 respectively.

m.c.izbudak@gmail.com

Characters

Liz and Zak — a retired couple in their late 60s.

Setting

A large high-ceilinged reception room in a dingy flat in West Kensington. The wallpaper and furniture seem dusty and nicotine stained. The air is stale. The audience must feel that the windows in that flat have not been opened for several years.

Two doors: one leading to the bedroom and the other leading to the hall and the front door.

An extended dining table in the middle of the room, one end of which has neatly stacked newspapers, magazines and books. The other end has dishes and remnants of a finished meal pushed to one edge to allow Liz to spread a pack of cards for a game of patience.

Liz is seated at the table pondering over a game of patience. She is obsessively systematic and ritualistic in the way she handles the cards.

Zak is sitting in an armchair with an ornate standard lamp behind him. He is staring at a newspaper crossword puzzle. Much of the time he is seated. From time to time he wanders aimlessly around the room and occasionally stands behind Liz scrutinising the game of patience.

It is almost 10 p.m.

LIZ	The news should be on soon.
ZAK	To have or to hold... To have or to hold within.
LIZ	*(She gathers the cards and then ritualistically shuffles them)* Seven letters?
ZAK	*(In a subdued tone)* Yes.
LIZ	*(She is staring at the cards and not looking at him)* Why do you insist on doing the easy puzzle? The news will be on in four minutes.
ZAK	Because I can't do the cryptic. And it's always the same bloody news.

	Today it will be: Day 3998 of the Crisis, Day 3967 of the State of Emergency.
LIZ	So, in two days' time we will be able to celebrate or commemorate — I prefer celebrate — 4000 days of the Crisis.
ZAK	We'll get an extra ration of coffee and loo paper, I suppose. The last time we got two 225g packet of special Colombian, which was definitely special, but I doubt whether it had ever been anywhere near Colombia. The loo paper was a memorable pink.
LIZ	I think that you are unduly cynical.
ZAK	And there will be a documentary about the Prime Minister's exemplary and heroic private life with shots of dogs, cats and lambs. That's what they always do.
LIZ	*(She looks up at him)* We will miss the headlines.
ZAK	And the Prime Ministerial statement. And a reiteration of the latest slogan: 'We will nip it in the bud together.' After all those school fees invested in him and the years of scholastic scrutiny of the *Iliad* and the *Aeneid*, that's all he can come up with? You don't 'nip things in the bud' — not after 4000 days.
LIZ	Three minutes have gone. He should have finished and the experts flanking him should now be talking.
ZAK	That way they can first blame the science and later the scientists. To have or to hold within.
LIZ	Fourth letter, 't'?
ZAK	You really irritate me.
LIZ	All those years of practice!
ZAK	I am not going to say anything. All right, what is it? *(Long pause as they stare at each other)* Well?

LIZ   Contain.

ZAK   It can't be that simple. *(Pause)*

LIZ   Another minute, and we will have a commercial break and a social message.

ZAK   With 'We will nip it in the bud together!' as the pervasive sub-moronic mantra.

LIZ   I really wish you did the cryptic crossword — you'd be so less irritable.

ZAK   We would all be less irritable, if we weren't in self-confinement — or, should I say, self-containment.

LIZ   Should be the sports news now.

ZAK   We haven't had any sports for those 3998 days! No football. No cricket. No rugby. Just repeats of old Grand Nationals, old FA Cup Finals and that old classic, the 1966 World Cup Final — black and white and grainy.

LIZ   Yes, but they are thinking ahead. According to the newspapers, they are thinking of combining and reviving the last three cancelled Olympics.

ZAK   And Olympic pigs can fly!

LIZ   You are so irritable.

ZAK   Of course I am irritable and irritated. We are confined to these walls, encased in this house, bound by the streets and the city.

LIZ   The country, continent, planet. Etcetera. Etcetera.

ZAK   The world is like a Russian doll — each doll is trapped within another bigger doll.

LIZ   You haven't surreptitiously had an extra ration of the sherry, have you?

ZAK   Doesn't life ever get you down?

LIZ   Oh, good.

ZAK   What?

LIZ	A black jack that can go on top of that red queen and then I can move that red ten. Things are looking up.

ZAK	Don't you ever feel down? Don't you feel trapped? Encased? Constrained?

LIZ	Contained?

ZAK	And death is no liberator. It's another constraint, another limitation.

LIZ	The finiteness of life is just a fact. Horrible word — finiteness. We only understand the finite — not the infinite. That's beyond our own realm.

ZAK	And the state of emergency. The endless self-quarantine. The years, the months, the days.

LIZ	3998 to be exact.

ZAK	How can you bear it?

LIZ	The fact is that we have never been free. We are all prisoners of time, mortgages, jobs and children. Even as students we had to think of exams and qualifications, and careers. As long as I had my pack of cards, the sherry and the odd bout of sex, I was immune to those externalities.

ZAK	I think I'm going to go for a walk.

LIZ	I didn't mind the kids. Actually, I quite liked them. As long as they grow up into decent human beings with a reasonable moral compass. *(Pause)* I've never really felt trapped.

ZAK	It can really get cold in the evenings.

LIZ	I've never made you feel trapped, have I?

ZAK	*(Pause)* Have I? I mean, have I ever made you feel trapped?

LIZ	As I said, as long as I had my sherry, my pack of cards and the odd bout of sex. *(She smiles as she moves some cards around)* The three of clubs comes to the rescue!

ZAK	I'm going to get my coat and scarf. *(Leaves the room)*
LIZ	I am happy not being unhappy. It certainly beats being unhappy about being unhappy.
ZAK	*(Offstage)* Do you think it is going to rain?
LIZ	*(Under her breath)* you never mention the kids, do you? *(Loudly)* Add the odd visit to the Royal Academy to the patience, sherry and sex.

Zak returns to the room wearing an overcoat and tying his scarf.

ZAK	I will be back in forty minutes or so.
LIZ	You know you can get arrested?
ZAK	I'll keep to the side streets.
LIZ	It's a State of Emergency until further notice.
ZAK	I'll be very careful. I'll make sure that nobody sees me.
LIZ	The law is the law.
ZAK	They say that street muggings are on the increase.
LIZ	Who says that?
ZAK	I heard it on the local news this morning.
LIZ	The ace of spades. About bloody time!
ZAK	Mind you — the weather forecast said that it was going to rain tonight.
LIZ	They always say that.
ZAK	Why would they?
LIZ	It's their default position. To hedge their bets.
ZAK	Mind you, I don't want to catch a cold.
LIZ	'Mind you', you are hovering with indecision.

ZAK   Mind you...

LIZ   Hovering has always been your problem... Three of spades... I had to propose to you and then I had to make you decide. It's a miracle that I didn't have to do your marriage vows for you.

ZAK   On the other hand *(pause)*.

LIZ   *(scrutinising her game of patience even more intensely)* This may actually work out.

ZAK   I'm not under any obligation, am I?

LIZ   What obligation is that?

ZAK   Actually, I think, I'll go for a walk tomorrow. *(Returns to his room)*

LIZ   Oh, and black five which would go nicely on top of that six of hearts. We could pour ourselves another ration of sherry. *(She stops the game waiting for a reaction. She takes a deep breath and repeats loudly)* We could pour ourselves an extra ration of sherry!

ZAK   *(Offstage)* Good idea. I'll try tomorrow. Might not be raining.

Liz is concentrating on her game of patience and humming under her breath an unrecognisable tune. Zak returns to watch the game of patience for a while, then goes back to his armchair, sits down and resumes his crossword puzzle.

LIZ   The weather forecast should be on soon.

ZAK   But we know what the weather is going to be.

LIZ   I know, but I still want to watch it.

ZAK   Apathy. Absence of hope.

LIZ   Are you talking about life or the weather forecast?

ZAK   12 down.

LIZ   Seven letters?

ZAK   *(In a subdued tone)* Yes, seven letters again.

LIZ	*(She continues staring at the cards and avoiding eye contact with him)* That's a really simple one. Why do you insist on doing the easy puzzle? The weather forecast will be on in four minutes.
ZAK	Answer to question one — as I've said before — because I can't do the cryptic. And... and what difference does it make whether we know the weather forecast or not, given that we have to stay indoors most of the time.
LIZ	Be patient. They will ease things sooner or later.
ZAK	This thing has been going on for 3998 days. *(Repeats empathically)* 3998.
LIZ	On Thursday we will be able to celebrate 4000 days of the Crisis.
ZAK	That would mean that it's Tuesday today and not Wednesday. *(Pause)* Can't be! *(Pause)* So what happened to Monday?
LIZ	If you mislaid Monday, that's your problem. The celebration, however, will be on Thursday.
ZAK	So we can look forward to that extra ration of coffee and loo paper, I suppose.
LIZ	We got an extra ration of sherry on day 2500, remember that?
ZAK	It was a bit sickly sweet.
LIZ	*(She looks up at him)* I think we've missed the weather forecast.
ZAK	Why this obsession with the weather forecast?
LIZ	Did you know that they get a special clothing allowance?
ZAK	So, the weather forecast is a sort of fashion show for you?
LIZ	It's not that — it's just interesting to see what they wear. What they spend their money on.

ZAK Good job they don't get performance pay.

LIZ Well, we missed it.

ZAK 12 down. Apathy and absence of hope.

LIZ Third letter, 's'?

ZAK I don't know. Now, what is 14 across? No, come to think of it, that would make sense.

LIZ Anyway, given that we don't have much to do apart from routine boredom, it'll be good to have a celebration on Thursday.

ZAK Celebrate what? The fact that we get an extra packet of loo paper? That we get an extra dose of bromidic broadcasts on TV?

LIZ Hold on, all I need is the eight of diamonds and I will have this game.

ZAK You know how much money the government saves because of the crisis? Think of all of us wrinklies staying at home, not travelling, we live in self-incarceration consuming fewer public services, we are made to feel guilty if we use the health system. Most of us will die of boredom or depression or both before we need to go to care homes or geriatric wards. While in the rest of the population: those who have jobs work under any conditions so as not to lose their jobs. The unemployed keep quiet in case they lose their benefits. While children and youngsters attend perpetual school getting brainwashed and intellectually castrated to be the next generation of call centre fodder.

Economically and politically this is perfect and it leaves them enough dosh to lower business taxes.

LIZ Time for a revolution?

ZAK Time for an extra sherry ration.

LIZ   Now that's a revolutionary idea!
ZAK   Despair?
LIZ   In a way, I suppose it is.
ZAK   No... 12 down?

BED-IN

(An extract from a short
play for the stage)

Written by

Imogen Lea

Imogen Lea is an emerging stage and screen writer from
Nottingham. With a keen interest in regional stories,
Imogen works to establish her own authentic voice. Through
her neurodiverse experience she uses detail and image to
conjure up complex, socially urgent and psychologically
rich worlds, while remaining playful and exploratory
with form.

imogen.lea@hotmail.co.uk

This play, written during the first lockdown in 2020, takes place in a set that looks like a plain-walled bedroom. However, the walls are electronic whiteboards/are projected. The tally marks that appear can be removed and replaced remotely. This piece is experimental and should be produced as an accessible performance.

PRE-SET:

MAN sits on the bed, watching WOMAN. As the audience enters, WOMAN writes tally marks on the wall in a black art pen. 1, 2, 3, 4, 5, 1, 2, 3, 4, 5 and so on. She keeps going until the audience is seated (there should be 50 marks). WOMAN and MAN undress and get into bed.

1. (50 marks)

MAN and WOMAN lying in bed, naked and embracing, a knot of two bodies, breathing heavily.

WOMAN Love you.

MAN I love you too.

They breathe.

WOMAN We don't have to do it every day. We're going to get tired of doing it every day.

MAN Doing it?

WOMAN We're going to get tired of it.

MAN I'm not.

He stands — puts on a dressing gown. She sits up.

WOMAN We should save it up.

MAN It's not going to run out.

WOMAN I know.

MAN I don't think.

He picks up two empty mugs.

WOMAN But if we just, all the time, it won't feel special, will it.

MAN Doesn't it feel special every time?

                                                                    112.

WOMAN   That's not what I mean. I just don't
             think we have to do it every day.
             Like there's nothing else to do.

MAN   But there isn't anything else to do.

The lights go off.

2. (1122 MARKS)

The lights come on.

WOMAN is asleep. MAN enters, silently. He listens to her breathing. He very carefully sits on his side of the bed, and reaches into his bedside drawer; he removes a box, opens it, and now holds a small vial and a hypodermic needle. He looks at WOMAN, then down at his hands. He breathes. He takes the vial, draws up the solution into the needle, and puts the vial down silently. He embraces WOMAN with one of his arms, kissing her neck, and then injects her carefully in her arm with his other hand. She does not stir. He puts the needle and the vial back in the drawer, and lies back, staring at the ceiling.

The lights slowly fade to total darkness.

3. (0 marks)

Lights come back on.

MAN and WOMAN are lying in bed asleep. A phone alarm rings on the MAN's side of the bed. WOMAN wakes up and crawls over MAN to turn it off. He wakes up and they struggle sleepily for the phone, he wins, and starts singing along to the alarm song. Eventually she breaks and joins in, they dance around their room, singing, laughing, playing, until they exhaust themselves. She collapses on the bed. He grabs a dressing gown and leaves, kissing the top of her head before he goes.

4. (55 MARKS)

WOMAN is lying in bed, uncomfortable. MAN shouts from outside the door.

MAN   (off) It says from concentrate?

WOMAN   (shouting) Then it won't work.

MAN   (off) But it's Ocean Spray — it's the nice one.

WOMAN   It doesn't matter if it's the nice one, it needs to be actual juice.

MAN   (off) It is.

WOMAN   It isn't, it's from concentrate.

He enters.

MAN   Well if it's not juice, what is it then?

WOMAN   I don't know.

They stare at each other.

MAN   Fine.

He leaves.

She picks at her fingernails. Thinks about biting them. Decides against it.

MAN   (off) There's blackcurrant squash? Will that help?

She says nothing.

He comes back in looking at a bottle of raspberry ketone pills — he sighs and throws them on the bed.

MAN   Should — I can go and get antibiotics — call the doctor and I think they'll let me pick them up from the pharmacy//

WOMAN   //No.

MAN   If it gets worse, then I'll need to get you some antibiotics//

WOMAN   //No. (she rips at her fingernails) It's too risky.

MAN   Risky?

WOMAN   Yes.

MAN   You know, everyone's getting used to new rules. They've got washing stations, there's markers on the floor in the Co-op. Telling people

                    where to stand, so they don't get
                    close y'know?

She rips too far down the nailbed and yelps in pain. He goes to her and sits on the bed.

MAN   What are you doing?

WOMAN   They're too long.

MAN   Well don't rip them, you weirdo.
                    I'll get you some scissors.

He gets up, and leans in to kiss her forehead; she flinches slightly. He makes for the door.

MAN   When did you stop biting them?

WOMAN   (pulling, wincing) What?

MAN   You bite your nails — you always
                    have.

WOMAN   (thinking) They might be dirty. I
                    don't want to put them in my mouth.

MAN   I suppose that makes sense — just
                    stop. Stop tearing at them! I'll get
                    you some scissors. Hang on.

He exits.

5. (0 MARKS)

WOMAN sits in bed. MAN enters with a new suit on; it looks ill-fitting and he is clearly uncomfortable.

MAN   It's not right.

WOMAN   It looks good.

MAN   Good?

WOMAN   It looks great.

MAN   Now I know you're lying.

WOMAN   I think it's very smart.

MAN   I'm wearing a tie.

WOMAN   I know, and it suits you. You look
                    like a football manager. Or a spy. Or
                    an accountant.

MAN	Very good.
WOMAN	You'll do fine, more than fine. You don't need to be nervous.
MAN	I'm not.
WOMAN	I can always tell — you get that wrinkle between your eyebrows. And your ears go pink.
MAN	They do not.
WOMAN	They do.

She runs over and puts her hands over his ears, facing him.

MAN	What are you—

She kisses him.

MAN	Thank you.
WOMAN	You're going to be great. But not that tie — wear the one you got for my sister's wedding, it's less 'accountanty'.
MAN	But I am an accountant OK. Wait there.

He exits.

6. SCENE (900 MARKS)

WOMAN sits in bed alone. She rocks, she doesn't know whether to hug her knees, or cover her head. She tries both. Neither helps.

7. (224 MARKS)

WOMAN is lying in bed. MAN enters. She sits up. Looks at him.

WOMAN	Oh.

She slumps.

MAN	Oh?
WOMAN	Did you make tea?

MAN   No.

She stares.

MAN   (sighing) Fine.

He exits.

8. (800 MARKS)

WOMAN stands staring at the wall. MAN enters, shirtless. He is wiping his left upper arm with a cotton ball covered in blue solution.

WOMAN   Why's it blue?

MAN   (smiling) it's just disinfectant.
         (he sits on the bed and she joins him)
         You don't need to look so worried.

WOMAN   But you don't know what you're doing.

MAN   They send you instructions. It's fine.

WOMAN   Now what. (she stands abruptly)

MAN   I need the rest of the postal kit.

She doesn't move.

MAN   I'll get it then.

He exits, she tears at her nails.

MAN   (entering with a needle in his hand, filled with a pale yellow liquid)
         It's very straightforward.

WOMAN   I'm not going to watch.

MAN   OK. (he sits again, she turns away)
         Sharp scratch. (he injects his arm)

WOMAN   It's not funny. Are you done?

MAN   (wincing) All done. See.

She touches the wall in front of her.

MAN   Shall I do yours?

WOMAN   I don't want it.

MAN	C'mon, we — we've talked about this.
WOMAN	Until we know, until there's some kind of feedback. More research. I'm not taking it.
MAN	(standing, sighing) Fine. I don't want to argue, not today. (he kisses the back of her head) We'll talk about it tomorrow. (he wipes his mouth) You should probably wash — you're, a bit, greasy.

He waits for her to turn and face him. She doesn't. She strokes the wall. He exits.

9. (300 MARKS)

WOMAN is lying in bed, reading an old history book. MAN is bouncing a tennis ball at the wall and catching it.

WOMAN	Did you know that...
MAN	What?
WOMAN	When Vesuvius erupted, and turned everyone to stone, their brains actually turned to glass.
MAN	Really?
WOMAN	Yeah.
MAN	How?
WOMAN	Dunno.
MAN	What?
WOMAN	I haven't read that bit yet.

She reads another page, and then puts the book in her lap.

WOMAN	When I die, can you turn my brain to glass, please?
MAN	You're not going to die.
WOMAN	I will one day.
MAN	It won't matter — I'm going to die first.
WOMAN	How'd you work that out?

MAN   You'll have sucked all the life out of me by then.

Lights go down.

10. (301 MARKS)

Lights up.

MAN now reads the same history book, while WOMAN, lying in bed, bounces the tennis ball on the ceiling.

MAN   You can get fired out of a cannon.
WOMAN   I don't want that.
MAN   Or diamonds, you can be a diamond.
WOMAN   No.
MAN   You could grow into a tree.
WOMAN   I want to be a paperweight or a vase.
MAN   That's silly.
WOMAN   You can drink from me.
MAN   That's weird.
WOMAN   You're weird.

Lights fade out.

11. (10 MARKS)

The lights have flickered back on.

MAN is in the bedroom, looking at the 10 MARKS on the wall.

WOMAN creeps around the door, wearing a surgical-style mask over her nose and mouth. She sneaks up behind him and taps him on the shoulder. He turns around and then jumps at her appearance.

MAN   Jesus.
WOMAN   (pulling mask down) What?
MAN   You look terrifying.
WOMAN   Well, we'll have to get used to it.

MAN	I suppose.

MAN turns back to face the marks on the wall. WOMAN hugs him from behind.

WOMAN	What do you think?
MAN	What's it for?
WOMAN	What do you mean? It's art, it's not *for* anything.
MAN	You mean in a few months when this is all over, you're going to cut out our bedroom wall and sell it as A Work Of Fine Art for thousands of pounds?
WOMAN	No. (she turns him around) Millions!

They kiss.

WOMAN	10 days, so 10 marks. Anyway, it won't be months, will it?

MAN removes her mask.

WOMAN	Will it?
MAN	I don't know. (he thinks) Are you worried?
WOMAN	Yes. No. No, not really. I am, only a bit — you know?
MAN	Yeah, I know. I'll make tea.

*MAN takes her hands and kisses them. He exits.
She stares at the marks.*

The lights flicker and then go out.

KING SIZE

(Radio sketch)

Written by

Hattie Manton

Hattie Manton is a comedy writer, who has experience in devising and acting primarily, with a BA in Drama at UEA. She is a Company Creative for Laughing Mirror Theatre where she helps create and workshop comedy scripts for their social media, as well as gets involved with devising scenes for performances.

H.manton@uea.ac.uk

King Size, is a short, silly, light-hearted radio sketch that represents the relatable female with the annoyingly high achiever best friend. Katherine comes to visit best friend Susan for a coffee and hits breaking point when she can't contain her jealousy, allowing all hell to break loose in front of her new crush.

CHARACTERS

KATHERINE: British, single mother (very single). She has let herself go rather. 50 but dresses like she's 70. Her constant struggle for money means she buys all her clothes from Oxfam and other charity shops. Never left the UK.

SUSAN: Katherine's best friend. American, has had a very successful life. Incredibly good-looking for her age. 49 but dresses like she's 20. Outgoing. Seen the world.

EMILY: 16. Waitress. 'Basic white girl'. Lovely eyeshadow.

GARY: Husky voice, well-spoken man.

INT. A SMALL VINTAGE CAFÉ, CAMBRIDGE

F/X: SOUNDS OF INAUDIBLE PEOPLE TALKING, GLASSES CLINKING. A FAINT BACKGROUND SOUND OF JAZZ MUSIC PLAYING CONTINUOUSLY TO SET THE SCENE OF THE CAFÉ. A FEW INTERLUDING TRAFFIC SOUND EFFECTS.

SUSAN	So dare I ask... how's the dating apps going?
KATHERINE	Oh God, Susie, you know me I'm awful with technology. I can't really get on with it, what on earth is a superlike?
SUSAN	It just takes a bit of getting used to. But Kath, you need to get yourself back out there, you're almost 50 now. I mean, you can't just rely on... Andrew the Asda man to sweep you off your feet!
KATHERINE	Who said I have a thing for Andy?
SUSAN	No one needs three grocery orders a week, Kath. Have you had any luck at all?
KATHERINE	With Andy?

SUSAN: No, with the apps!

KATHERINE: Oh right, well there is this one chap who has shown an interest. Gary...

SUSAN: Ooooo let's see!

F/X: UNLOCKING OF PHONE

SUSAN: Kath!! He's saucy... Gary Goodman... More like Gary Good-lookin'! (LAUGHS) Local too?

KATHERINE: Yes. I know. Never mind a snack, he's quite the full meal, isn't he?

SUSAN: Why have you only just mentioned Gorgeous Gaz?

KATHERINE: I don't know, he seems a bit kinky for me though, following our date. I left that side of me in my thirties.

SUSAN: KINKY? Come on Kath, this seems like the perfect opportunity for you? I mean it must have been, what, three years now since you last got some... action... Some (TERRIBLE BRITISH ACCENT) rumpy pumpy, lil bit of sauce... for that dry ole bun of yours... Some coins in your ole, crusty jukebox to get it playing that sweet sweet music?

AWKWARD BEAT.

Catch my drift? I mean, come on Kath. I've had two kids since then... and a lot of (CLOSE) king-size cock...

KATHERINE: You know you can just mention Paul's cock without referring to the size, don't you?

SUSAN: Hey, you know I would if I could it's just... eight years of marriage and still BAM! amazes me every time. (LOW) So muscular.

KATHERINE (COUGHS)

SUSAN: Anyway, my point is surely you must be absolutely gagging for some/

KATHERINE	(INTERRUPTS) /Yes, thank you Susie for reminding me of my loneliness, once again.
SUSAN	All I'm saying is you should give this Gary a try! Just to get yourself back out there! What's stopping you?!
KATHERINE	(CLOSE) He wants phone sex.
SUSAN	(LOUD) What?!
KATHERINE	He's asked if we can have phone sex.
SUSAN	(PAUSE) DO IT!
KATHERINE	I don't know how to be sexy over the phone! The only people I call are you and Asda customer services...
SUSAN	Kath. This is how it's done these days! Trust me. I mean to be honest, sometimes I wish I was still single to get back out there and do crazy things like that... but I'm unfortunately way too comfortable with my life to even dream of—

<u>F/X: SOUNDS OF LIQUID BEING POURED AND PLATES BEING PILED UP</u>

WAITRESS	Hey! Sorry to interrupt, ladies, there is a special today for mothers and daughters? Half price on all our afternoon teas.
SUSAN	Oh... thank you?
WAITRESS	So I can get that taken off your bill for you and Mum.
KATHERINE	Oh no... we're not mother and daughter.
WAITRESS	Oh wow, sorry... grandma, you just look young for your age! Well the deal still app—
KATHERINE	(SMALL SARCASTIC LAUGH) Not related. Just friends. Same age. In fact she's actually two months younger than me.
WAITRESS	Oh right, well...(CLEARS THROAT) Enjoy your tea cakes, ladies.
SUSAN	Thank you. I love your eyeshadow!

F/X: SOUND OF SLURPING LIQUID, FOOTSTEPS GETTING DISTANT

SUSAN Don't take it personally... she's only young.

KATHERINE Don't take it personally? She just tried to call me your grandma. Do I really look that old?

SUSAN Maybe the scarf isn't doing much for you. That's all I'll say. Yellow is no one's colour.

KATHERINE Shut up, Susie. It must be all right for you, mustn't it, all married with your happy family and country cottage, life sorted. But yet still looking 31 with your fresh highlights in, your flared trousers and turtle neck that somehow suits you. Oh of course you suit turtle necks, who the hell suits turtle necks?! Coming out for brunch with your embarrassment of a best friend who shouldn't have worn the bloody scarf because (EXAGGERATED AMERICAN ACCENT)'Yellow is no one's colour.' Well, I'm sorry Susie, my neck was fucking chilly.

SUSAN Hey Kath... I didn't mean it like that... Please don't do this again.

KATHERINE That's easy for you to say, isn't it! Oooo look at me, I'm such an easy-going cool 'mom' who has Instagram and gets called a 'milf' in the school car park and still gets asked out in bars but it's just so hard for me because I have to turn them all down for my big daddy cock at home that is KING SIZE. Did I mention that? Did I mention the size of my husband's cock? Oh wait, yeah I did every day for fucking eight years!

FX: INAUDIBLE SOUNDS OF CHATTER LOWER

SUSAN Hey Kath, I'm sorry she thought you were a lil' older; let's just drop this. You are causing a scene. Tell me more about Gary.

KATHERINE   Oh I'm causing a scene am I? God
            forbid I embarrass you Susie and
            your perfect reputation! What's the
            problem? Grandma making you feel
            uncomfortable?

WAITRESS   Is every thing all right over here?

SUSAN   Hey yes, sorry, she's fine. This
            happens a lot. We'll leave.

F/X: CHAIR SCRAPING ACROSS FLOOR

KATHERINE   I'm quite happy here actually. You
            might need to fetch me some wheels
            before I leave anyway, grandma bones
            you know, quite the struggle to get
            around!

SUSAN   Sorry about her... Come on Kath, let's
            bounce!

KATHERINE   You know what, Sus... you should
            be jealous of me and my phone sex
            appointment. I bet Gary's got it all
            going for him downstairs, never mind
            king size, we are talking monster
            cock... I bet I won't be able to walk
            for days, then I'll really need that
            wheelchair for my... painful stretched
            arse VAGINA...

WAITRESS   I'm going to have to ask you to
            leave. Customers are starting to feel
            uncomfortable.

F/X: SCRAPING OF PAPER ACROSS A TABLE

KATHERINE   Oh. And you can just shove that
            coffee bill right up your arse!

SUSAN   Katherine...

KATHERINE   Or maybe shove it up Susie's arse
            right next to where your head seems
            to be. Don't blame you though.
            There's a lot of heads down there.
            Gotta be one wide arsehole. Not a
            pretty sight, if you ask me.

SUSAN	Katherine, stop...
KATHERINE	Now tell me...
WAITRESS	Emily.
KATHERINE	OUCH. Emily? That's a really basic name, I feel for you. Do you often go around here assuming women my age are grandmas, Emily? (CLOSE)
EMILY	(TREMBLING) It was just a mistake!
KATHERINE	Is that what gives you the kick in life? Well, let me tell you, you ain't going far in life if it is. You're lucky I'm strong and I can handle crushing comments like that. Others wouldn't be so thick-skinned... But let me tell you something, Emsy...
SUSAN	(THROUGH TEETH) Katherine, people are looking.
KATHERINE	I am Katherine Carter, an attractive, empowered woman who can do whatever she fucking wants. And that's why I'm having phone sex with this sexy man tonight. (PAUSE)

F/X: UNLOCKING OF PHONE SOUND EFFECT. GASPS FROM SPECTATORS IN THE CAFÉ. THE BACKGROUND CHATTER BECOMES WHISPERS.

KATHERINE	Get a load of that. Good-looking, isn't he? Gary Goodman has a bloody good PENIS.

F/X: BACKGROUND SOUNDS OF CHATTER COME TO AN AWKWARD HALT

KATHERINE	Now do you think I'm a grandma, pink eyes?
WAITRESS	URGHHH!

F/X: SOUND OF DOOR OPENING AND FOOTSTEPS GETTING CLOSER

GARY	Katherine?

KATHERINE Gary... what are you doing here?

GARY Katherine, I...

KATHERINE (FLUSTERED) Please I can explain, I just had a bit of bad service that's all...

GARY Emily, I'll wait in the car.

WAITRESS OK, Dad.

F/X: DOOR CLOSING

KATHERINE Dad? Oh fuck me. OF COURSE. OF COURSE this would happen to me! Emily... Goodman then, is it?

WAITRESS You got it. Tina... I'm clocking out.

TINA (OFF) OK, thank you sweetheart, see you tomorrow!

WAITRESS Bye, Katherine Carter. (CLOSE) For the record... my dad's married.

SUSAN Damn.

KATHERINE Well, this is highly awkward now.

SUSAN Don't sweat it, I know the mix of caffeine and sugar sometimes goes to your head a lil... Gary probably wasn't all that.

KATHERINE Well, I think I'll just go home and do another Asda delivery – we're out of milk.

SUSAN OK Kath. Same time next week?

KATHERINE Sure. (CLOSE) Different café though?

SUSAN I think so.

END.

WOMAN

(Short Film)

Written by

Louise Pesery

Louise Pesery is a French scriptwriter. She is completing
the MA Scriptwriting at the University of East Anglia.
Louise has a true passion for screenwriting, and a strong
desire to develop stage plays. She also aspires to be a
filmmaker, and has already written, directed, and edited
three short movies.

louise.pesery@hotmail.fr

The scene takes place in the Musée d'Orsay in Paris, in the room where is displayed L'Origine du monde (The Origin of the world) by Gustave Courbet.

In the background on the right, is sitting the MUSEUM ATTENDANT. A couple enters, CAMILLE and CHARLIE. Camille observes the painting while Charlie tries to look away.

CAMILLE	What do you see?
CHARLIE	What?
CAMILLE	The painting. What do you see?
CHARLIE	Paint.
CAMILLE	Come on, look at it. What do you see?
CHARLIE	It's just a random painting, Cam.
CAMILLE	That is precisely the opposite of a random painting, Charlie.

Charlie looks around, embarrassed.

CAMILLE	So tell me, what do you see?
CHARLIE	Why are you even asking me that?
CAMILLE	Because it's important for me? I'd like to know what you think of it.
CHARLIE	A pussy.
CAMILLE	I'm sorry?
CHARLIE	I see a pussy.
CAMILLE	Very elegant.
CHARLIE	You asked me.
CAMILLE	I see a real woman.
CHARLIE	Great.
CAMILLE	A true body.
CHARLIE	If you say so.
CAMILLE	This is... art... pure art... art at its finest.
CHARLIE	Are you done?
CAMILLE	You're the pussy here.
CHARLIE	Excuse me?
CAMILLE	You don't have the balls to look at the painting.

CHARLIE	I'm not gonna look at some hairy pussy! This is disturbing.
CAMILLE	You think a woman's vagina is disturbing?
CHARLIE	Can you just... Keep it down? We're in a freaking museum.
CAMILLE	You think a woman's vagina is disturbing? Is my vagina disturbing?
CHARLIE	Stop twisting my words. I'm just saying... this... this painting... is disturbing. It's inappropriate.
CAMILLE	The painting isn't inappropriate. It's what you are projecting on the painting that is inappropriate.
CHARLIE	Why did you make me come here in the first place, huh?

Camille stays silent.

CHARLIE	Cam? Hello? I asked you a question.
CAMILLE	I know.
CHARLIE	Answer then!

Beat.

CAMILLE	I think I want to break up with you.
CHARLIE	What?
CAMILLE	I'm sorry.
CHARLIE	You think? What does that even mean?
CAMILLE	I want to break up with you.
CHARLIE	No, you said, you think you want to break up with me. That's different, Cam.
CAMILLE	No, I'm sorry I do.
CHARLIE	No you don't.
CAMILLE	I do.
CHARLIE	Cam, this is ridiculous, just because we have an argument about some stupid painting it doesn't mean that we need to break up.
CAMILLE	It's not a stupid painting, Charlie!

CHARLIE: It is! Why are you so attached to this painting? What's wrong with you?

CAMILLE: What's wrong with me?

She takes a deep breath.

CAMILLE: I always wanted to see this painting in real life. You know, not just on my computer screen. I wanted to see all the details, the texture, how the light reflects on it... I've lived in Paris for six years now, and I never took the time to come here. But I guess Parisians never take the time for anything... It made me realise so much about women's conditions: how the society sees us, treats us, objectifies us... So I wanted to come here with you. Because I think it is very important for you to see it, to take a good look at it. I'm sure you can learn a lot from it. And I guess I wanted to prove to myself that I needed to break up with you. Because if you can't see what I see, well... we can't be together.

CHARLIE: You're breaking up with me because of a painting?

CAMILLE: You know it's funny because you like it when I send you nudes, but somehow you find this inappropriate.

CHARLIE: Nudes are not something you put on a wall in a museum.

CAMILLE: Why is that?

CHARLIE: Because it's fucking voyeurism, Cam!

The museum attendant is looking at Charlie and Camille; he clears his throat loudly. Charlie apologises by making a gesture with his hands.

CAMILLE: A lot of people like voyeurism. I'm sure some people look at it and are turned on.

CHARLIE: Yeah, maybe in the 18th century.

CAMILLE: This is a painting from the 19th century.

CHARLIE   Whatever. This is not sexy. She's clearly overweight and she has a lot of pubic hair. This is gross.

CAMILLE   So you're saying that a hairless, skinnier body is more attractive?

CHARLIE   Yes.

CAMILLE   So basically, you are describing a little girl's body, not a woman's body.

CHARLIE   You're twisting my words again.

CAMILLE   I'm really not though... See that's the problem. You are a product of this society, so you have inappropriate expectations of a woman's body. And because men have these expectations, women feel like they need to comply with these in order to be attractive to a man's eyes. And as many women, for many years, I committed to it. I shaved and waxed my entire body for you to find me sexy. I dressed up and wore uncomfortable clothes to get your attention. I wear make-up every fucking day even though I didn't need it just because I was afraid you would think I was not pretty enough.

Beat.

CAMILLE   Come on — say something!

CHARLIE   I...

Beat.

CHARLIE   I didn't realise you had so much pressure...

CAMILLE   Now I get it.

CHARLIE   What?

CAMILLE   I understand why you never made me cum.

Charlie glances at the museum attendant, hoping he didn't hear what Camille just said. But he did.

CHARLIE   I'm sorry?

CAMILLE   You know nothing about women.

CHARLIE   I am a great lay.

CAMILLE   You're not.

CHARLIE   Why did you scream my name and make those moans during sex, then? Why did you scratch my back? Why the hell did you say 'that was fucking good' after we just had sex?

CAMILLE   Because I was faking it.

CHARLIE   You faked it?

CAMILLE   Some women fake all their life.

Charlie stays quiet and stares at the painting.

CAMILLE   You know, a few months ago, a woman was refused entry as she was wearing a low-necked summer dress. They said that her outfit was inappropriate to enter a museum. This is very ironic for such a place to refuse entry to a woman because of her clothes and on another side to display a painting of a woman's vulva. I don't know why people are so afraid of a woman's body.

Camille looks at Charlie, still staring at the painting.

CAMILLE   I wish you had looked at my vagina as you are looking at this one.

Beat.

CAMILLE   What do you see now?

CHARLIE   My... mistakes?

CAMILLE   Don't blame yourself, you are a man raised in a patriarchal society.

Charlie gets closer to the painting.

CHARLIE   Who is she?

CAMILLE   I think they found her identity two or three years ago. But I don't really think who she is matters. She's all of us.

CHARLIE   Does yours look like that?

CAMILLE   See, that's the problem, you should have known that.

CHARLIE   Are you breaking up with me because I'm... a man?

CAMILLE   I'm breaking up with you because you have never considered me as your equal.

They stare at the painting in silence for a while.

CHARLIE   Is it still necessary to display this... here?

CAMILLE   Why is it so difficult for you to put it into words? You only refer to it by saying 'this' or 'pussy', why do you have issues with using the v-word?

CHARLIE   The v-word?

CAMILLE   Vagina.

Charlie, embarrassed, looks around them and catches the eye of the museum attendant.

CHARLIE   No one uses it. It's like a medical word.

CAMILLE   A medical word?

CHARLIE   Yeah. A word that doctors would use.

CAMILLE   That's bullshit.

CHARLIE   What is the point of all this? I mean, beside giving you entitlement for dumping me?

CAMILLE   Actually... Before coming here, I rehearsed everything I wanted to tell you. I wanted to force you to become aware of your unconscious misogyny. Because in the end, you are a good guy and I truly loved you and... I still want what's best for you...

CHARLIE   Are you kidding me?

CAMILLE   What?

CHARLIE   So this whole thing was a fucking show that you rehearsed?

CAMILLE I'm sorry, I didn't mean to say it like that.

CHARLIE You're such a selfish know-it-all bitch.

Beat.

CHARLIE I love you.

CAMILLE Don't.

CHARLIE I do.

CAMILLE Please don't.

CHARLIE Don't you love me?

CAMILLE Not anymore.

Camille leaves the stage. Charlie stays in front of the painting. A WOMAN enters and stands next to Charlie. He notices her, gets closer.

CHARLIE *Did you know, a woman was refused entry as she was wearing a low-necked dress? They said that her outfit was inappropriate. How ironic, huh? To refuse entry to a woman because of her clothes but to have a painting of a woman's vagina displayed. I don't know why people are so afraid of a woman's body, when it's just art... pure art... art at its finest.*

ANGLE

(A Short Film)

Written by

Rosalie Pratt

Rosalie is a writer for screen and stage currently studying on UEA's Scriptwriting MA. She enjoys writing true-to-life characters while exploring the flexibility of space and time. She works as an Editorial Assistant, which rarely coincides with her scriptwriting aspirations.

rosaliejoy127@gmail.com

EXT. PARTY — NIGHT

Flashing lights stream out of the windows of a three-storey house, illuminating the quiet countryside road. Pop music blares out of speakers, muffled singing and shouting coming from within.

Dim light pours through an open skylight on the roof, next to which sit JAMES, 18, and ANNA, 17.

EXT. ROOF — CONTINUOUS

Anna is put together in her hair and outfit — just jeans and a nice top — but some of her make-up has sweated off throughout the night. James has messy hair and a pensive face.

Anna keeps glancing over at James, waiting for him to say something. Her mind wanders and she surveys the people mingling below.

Anna laughs to herself.

                    JAMES
What?

                    ANNA
This is the first party I've been to in ages.

                    JAMES
And?

Anna checks her phone. The time reads 00:10AM. She smiles.

                    ANNA
I'd normally have finished work by now and be asleep in bed.

                    JAMES
Dreaming about how much fun we're all having at these parties?

Anna scoffs.

                    ANNA
Fuck off.

JAMES
You're missing out though. And we miss you when you're not here.

ANNA
You know it's not up to me. Work has me down for Friday and Saturday shifts.

JAMES
Why?

ANNA
What? Why do I have a job?

James nods. Anna looks up at the stars as she thinks. A sad realisation washes over her.

ANNA (CONT'D)
I'm lonely. At home, I mean. The house doesn't feel right without Carrie. At least it's only a term abroad; she'll be back soon.

A beat.

ANNA (CONT'D)
I guess I'm just home alone a lot now. Parents are always out.

A longer beat.

ANNA (CONT'D)
Why are we talking about this? I thought absinthe was supposed to knock you out?

JAMES
I haven't stolen it yet, just on cider for now. Also stolen though.

They both laugh.

Anna looks down at the party below, people hug each other in the driveway as they arrive.

ANNA
I want to be drunk. Feel out of it.

                    JAMES
          That sounds suspicious... like you
          have secrets.

He punches her arm, but she's deep in thought, still watching the party below. People have started to notice that they're on the roof.

                    ANNA
          You get drunk quite a lot.

                    JAMES
          I guess. More than you anyway.

                    ANNA
          Why do you do it?

A beat.

                    JAMES
          Helps me think.

                    ANNA
          What if you don't remember what you
          were thinking?

                    JAMES
          Sometimes you just know that you
          came to a productive conclusion.

                    ANNA
          Is that going to happen tonight?

                    JAMES
          You're the one that's never
          been drunk and so can remember
          everything, you tell me.

                    ANNA
          Beer and cider, you open up more.
          Don't know about absinthe though.

                    ANNA (CONT'D)
          James?

                    JAMES
          Yeah?

                    ANNA
          I shouldn't be the one you open up to.

James shrugs.

JAMES
Well, I don't know where she is right now.

ANNA
I'm not talking about tonight!

JAMES
Then what are you talking about?

ANNA
I'm talking about every night! Your girlfriend already thinks I'm in love with you, being your confidante doesn't exactly help with that. That's why I took that sodding awful job, so I'm always busy at the weekends. It isn't about being bored, or my sister, or my parents, it's... *you*.

JAMES
I knew we were going to end up like this eventually.

ANNA
James—

JAMES
—I'd never tell you. It was always going to be you that brought it up. Which is surprising since, like you said, you're rarely here and never drunk. It was always going to be you. She's going to kill me. I love her and she loves me but she's practically terrified of you.

James seems genuinely upset. Anna laughs quietly.

JAMES (CONT'D)
Anna!

ANNA
Sorry, it's just that you'd laugh too if you could see the irony.

James glares at Anna. She explains herself, the irony being

overwhelmed by Anna's growing anger.

ANNA (CONT'D)
You get drunk and you open up about this stuff. You tell me things and it makes me uncomfortable but that's why you have that productive feeling afterwards! Deep down you know that bottling everything up doesn't do anything. You don't have some part of your subconscious that you unlock when you're drunk, it's just me, I just talk to you. For fuck's sake, James, I'm the one that gets asked if I'm in love with you when you're the one that treats me like his fucking girlfriend!

James stares at Anna, surprised at her outburst.

ANNA (CONT'D)
I — I think I'm gonna go. Yeah, that makes sense. I'll see you on Monday, I guess.

Before she can get up, James pulls Anna into a firm hug. She settles into it.

ANNA (CONT'D)
We've been friends for so long. I didn't mean to get angry like this.

ANNA (CONT'D)
You're still my best friend, you know?

She plays with the hair on the nape of his neck. They press their foreheads together and smile feebly.

EXT. PARTY — CONTINUOUS

A few people watch them embrace from below. Somebody takes a photo. From this angle, it looks as if James and Anna are kissing.

INT. SECOND FLOOR LANDING — LATER

Anna sits on the floor. She wipes her eyes and smudges more of her make-up. Her eyes widen.

She rushes over to a mirror and takes deep, shaky breaths as she removes a pair of contact lenses.

Anna takes out her phone out and, squinting, types:

MESSAGE TO: Mum
    'Hey, I'm ready to be picked up'

She ends the text with a love heart and closes her phone.

A text from Mum immediately pops up 'On my way, love! X'

The time reads 00:23AM.

Audible above the music is the sound of a girl wailing and a door slamming.

CUT TO:

EXT. DRIVEWAY — NIGHT

Anna sits on a bench next to a long, gravel driveway. The music drowns out girls talking nearby but she still notices people whispering to each other as they switch between looking at her and the photo.

She checks her phone. 00:27AM.

The group of people nearby are still staring at Anna, except now they are leaning into a phonecall. One of the girls, a shortish brunette in a glittery party dress, nods and hangs up the phone.

Anna squints as she attempts to recognise the girls. She can't see them properly without her contacts. She taps her foot nervously.

The sound of tyres crunching over gravel, the gossipers disperse as Anna's mum pulls up in her hatchback.

Anna hops up and moves quickly to the car door. She looks up at the roof; James is still there, staring into the night.

INT. CAR — CONTINUOUS

Anna fakes a yawn as she settles into the passenger seat.

The gossipers walk down the quiet country road at the end of the drive.

EXT. ROOF — NIGHT

James sits on the roof and fiddles with his hands. His phone lights up from inside his pocket but he doesn't notice.

The music on the speakers changes to a song James likes. Tempted by the music, he jumps through the skylight and back into the party.

INT. LANDING — CONTINUOUS

James lands. His eyes fixate on the bottom drawer of a chest of drawers, the top of which is covered in birthday cards and bunches of flowers.

James rummages around in the drawer before pulling out a bottle full of green liquid. The label is faded but words faintly remain – *La Fée Absinthe*.

He takes a few gulps before running into a nearby room and slamming the door.

INT. LANDING — MOMENTS LATER

James returns to the landing, wiping spit off his mouth.
The absinthe has hit him like a train.

INT. FIRST FLOOR — CONTINUOUS

James makes his way past people kissing on beds or throwing up in toilets, and goes through the house into the kitchen downstairs.

INT. GROUND FLOOR — KITCHEN — CONTINUOUS

This seems to be the hub of the party, but the jovial atmosphere lulls for a moment as James enters.

James sees JAKE, 18, across the kitchen. James picks up a cider from the side and 'cheers'-es Jake.

Jake violently gestures towards the front door of the house, signalling James to leave.

Jake quickly taps at his phone and James's flashes in his pocket.

Jake points at his phone and then at James. He waves it in the air but he's knocked by a drunk girl stumbling by and the phone goes flying.

James rolls his eyes and finally checks his phone. A notification from Jake appears, as do thirteen missed calls from 'Cara <3'.

He opens the message from Jake.
'TROUBLE. Get out of here.'

Confused, James does a quick self-pat down. Phone, yes, it's in his hand. Keys, no. Wallet, no.

James thinks for a moment but can't remember where they might be. He downs the cider and groans before bolting upstairs.

INT. FIRST FLOOR — CONTINUOUS

He goes for the first door he sees when he reaches the top of the stairs.

INT. BEDROOM — CONTINUOUS

The master bedroom. Four-poster bed, chandelier, a well-lit en suite visible in the far corner.

Two people are having sex on the bed. They scream as James enters.

At the foot of the bed, placed on an ornate red and gold ottoman, is a bowl of keys. James grimaces and looks back at the couple, who have resumed noisily having sex. He hopes the bowl is there as a joke.

He fishes through the bowl of keys until he reaches his. He shakes his head as he puts the bowl of keys back.

INT. LANDING — MOMENTS LATER

James looks around, figuring out which door to go through next.

He decides on an odd-looking dark door. Shouting comes from within.

INT. GAMES ROOM — MOMENTS LATER

A 20-strong group of people crowd around a stained snooker table being used for beer pong. Again, the party atmosphere temporarily lulls when James enters.

He pushes his way through the crowd to the edge of the table and spots his wallet, nested in the far side pocket of the table.

He runs around the table in time to be splashed by a grubby ping-pong ball entering a plastic cup of beer as he reaches for his wallet before leaving the room quickly.

EXT. ROAD — LATER

James walks down the dark country lane, the music still audible in the background.

From seemingly out of nowhere the gossipers, including the short brunette and a taller, crying blonde, CARA, 18, appear.

Cara steps towards him, her shaking hands holding out a phone showing the photo of him and Anna on the roof. James's jaw drops as he looks at the photo, confused. He knows he didn't kiss Anna.

James opens his mouth to explain himself, but before he can the short brunette punches him in the face.

The group of girls moves towards him as he stumbles back and falls.

All of the girls except Cara take turns hitting or kicking James, his cries of pain growing louder. They stop after a while and step back, allowing Cara to come forward.

> JAMES
> Cara! Please, listen to me! It's the angle... I'd never do that. I know you don't like...

She's furious but finds the strength to curb stomp James, who lies on the floor, motionless.

Cara starts sobbing as she and the group walk away from James and the party and into the night. James lies on the ground, his head bleeding gently.

All of a sudden, police sirens sound in the distance and the music from the party shuts off.

The crowd disperses. A few people walk past James, but nobody seems to notice him. He just looks like he's drunkenly passed out on the road.

As the last of the partygoers leave the area, James, upon seeing flashing lights drawing near, drags himself to his feet.

His head pounds as he balances himself, he closes his eyes when he sees his bloodied hand that was once holding his head.

James stumbles into the road, waving his bloody hands feebly as police cars storm down the road.

END

BUT WHAT DID THEY ACTUALLY DO?

(Extract from play)

Written by

Lindsay Sharman

Lindsay Sharman has worked as a performer, writer and producer for over ten years. In 2020 she set up the audio drama company, Long Cat Media (www.longcatmedia.com). Lindsay is the writer and director of audio dramas *Mockery Manor*, *The Ballad of Anne & Mary*, and *Madame Magenta*.

ljsharman@yahoo.com

A dormitory with four beds, four bedside tables, and four wardrobes.

Three of the bed-spaces have been personalised with teddy bears, trinkets and posters. A radio sits on a bedside table, playing pop hits from the 70s, 80s and 90s.

In the fourth space, the bed is stripped and the walls are bare — no one lives here.

Alex, **Caz** *and* **Emma**, *aged seventeen, are sprawled across this empty bed-space. They have an air of studied nonchalance.* **Caz** *is perched on the bedside table, reading a magazine.* **Alex** *leans against the headboard, picking at her cuticles.* **Emma** *hangs off the bed, examining her hair for split ends.*

The distant flushing of a toilet, followed by the sound of approaching footsteps. The three girls share a look — the games are about to begin — and then return to their activities.

Susan *enters the room. She's smiling.*

SUSAN   Hi!

Emma *continues to examine her split ends.* **Caz** *reads.* **Alex** *is the only one who looks up, face blank.*

Susan's *smile falters.*

SUSAN   I'm new. Clearly! I'm Susan. *(beat)* Oh, is this bed taken? I thought it was free so I put my bag...

Susan *looks for her suitcase. It's where she left it that morning: by the bedside table.* **Caz** *is using it as a footrest.*

     ...there. Sorry, can I..? Just need to get to it. Thanks. Sorry!

Susan *slides her suitcase out from under the girl's feet.* **Caz** *looks up from her magazine, frowning.*

ALEX   Do you want us to move?

SUSAN   No, no! That's cool.

After a moment's hesitation, **Susan** *turns to the wardrobe and opens the door. A single T-shirt hangs from the rail. Otherwise, it is glaringly empty.*

*At this evidence of occupancy, **Susan** closes the wardrobe door.*

SUSAN   I think I must be in the wrong dorm. I'll just... go check...

***Susan** exits, suitcase in hand.*

***Emma** gives a snort of stifled laughter. **Alex** grins and hits her.*

ALEX   Shut up!

CAZ   Should we tell her?

***Alex** stretches like a cat, before crossing the room to her portable stereo.*

ALEX   Nah. Stay there. She'll be back in a minute. Go turn the music up, Caz.

CAZ   Yes, your majesty.

Caz goes to her bedside table and cranks the volume on her radio. Eric Carmen's 'Hungry Eyes' fills the room.

***Alex** dances to the music, exaggerating the moves to amuse **Caz** and **Emma**. They laugh. **Caz** wolf-whistles.*

***Susan** appears in the doorway. **Alex** continues to dance, but with more languid movements.*

SUSAN   All the beds are taken.

***Alex** shakes her head as if she can't hear her. **Susan** takes a step into the room, raises her voice above the music.*

SUSAN   The other dorms are full. I think this is my bed. Do you know whose shirt is in the wardrobe?

***Alex** doesn't answer. Instead, she walks over to the radio and pointedly turns it off.*

ALEX   What?

SUSAN   There's a shirt in the wardrobe?

ALEX   Oh my God, a shirt in a wardrobe! Call the police!

***Caz** and **Emma** giggle. **Susan** forces herself to laugh along.*

EMMA   It's mine.

SUSAN   Oh, OK! Cool!

EMMA   My wardrobe is full.

CAZ   Emma's got loads of clothes. Spoilt bitch.

Emma gives Caz the finger.

SUSAN   Do you... want it back?

Emma frowns at Susan.

EMMA   My wardrobe is full. It won't fit.

SUSAN   Right, yeah. No problem!

Susan unzips her suitcase. She takes out her own clothes and starts to fill the wardrobe, gently nudging Emma's shirt to the side.

SUSAN   I'm Susan, by the way.

ALEX   Hi Susan-by-the-way.

Hoping this is a crumb of friendship, Susan jumps on it.

SUSAN   Are you Alex?

ALEX   Yeah. How did you know?

SUSAN   Mr Bromley said you were in my dorm—

ALEX   *(interrupts)* Bromley hates me. Why are you so late? Term started three days ago.

CAZ   I get in trouble when I'm late. Bromley hates me too.

EMMA   No he doesn't. He fancies you, the old perv. Stares at your tits.

CAZ   At least I have some.

Caz looks at Susan's chest. Susan folds her arms, then unfolds them.

ALEX   Why're you late, then?

SUSAN   Something came up.

ALEX   Oh yeah? What?

SUSAN   *(quiet)* Just... personal stuff.

ALEX	Like what?
SUSAN	(*quieter*) Just a medical thing.
ALEX	You're so quiet! I can't hear you!
SUSAN	(*loud*) A medical thing. It's nothing.
EMMA	Erg! Is it contagious?
SUSAN	No!
ALEX	What was it then?
SUSAN	It was nothing, really...
EMMA	Don't tell us! We can guess! Yay, fun game!

'Fun game' has a Pavlovian effect on the three girls.

They've clearly done this before, to the extent they've developed a cute little routine.

ALEX	Fun game! Fun game!
CAZ	Fun game! Fun game!
EMMA	I'll go first.
CAZ	You always go first.
EMMA	Diphtheria.
ALEX	What the fuck is diphtheria?
EMMA	I dunno.
CAZ	Well how do you know she's got it, then? My turn.
SUSAN	No, don't. It's really boring, anyway.

Caz *studies* **Susan.**

SUSAN	I don't really want to play—
CAZ	(*interrupts*) —Shhh! Herpes.
ALEX	Don't be stupid. You have to have had sex to get herpes.
CAZ	No you don't! Cold sores are herpes. My dad kissed me with a cold sore when I was a baby and now I get them—
ALEX	(*interrupts*) —Urgh, stop snogging your dad.
CAZ	I don't snog my dad!

EMMA: Oh my God, your dad gave you an STD!

CAZ: It's oral herpes! It's not—

EMMA: *(shrieking)* Oral herpes! You dirty cow! Get away from me!

Emma *draws her feet up to her chest, away from Caz.*

CAZ: It's just cold sores! Ugh, you're so — just shut up!

EMMA: I borrowed your toothpaste! Gross! Oh my God, Caz, if you've given me—

ALEX: Both of you, shut UP. Seriously. You're so childish.

Emma *and* **Caz** *quieten down.* **Caz** *gives* **Emma** *one last kick across the bedspread.*

EMMA: *(Hisses)* Don't touch me.

Alex *shoots them a warning look.*

ALEX: Anyway, she missed the start of term. It's more serious than herpes. Let me think. Hmmm.

Alex *looks at* **Susan**, *considering.*

SUSAN: *(Scared)* It's really not that interesting.

ALEX: So just tell us then. Why make it a big deal.

SUSAN: It's private.

There's an intake of breath from **Caz** *and* **Emma**. *Nobody says no to* **Alex**.

ALEX: *(cold)* I think we have a right to know, Susan. We're sharing a dorm with you. Have you considered how we feel? If you *have* something—

SUSAN: *(interrupts)* Honestly, it's nothing. You can't catch it... I wasn't ill.

EMMA: But you just said you were. So you were lying?

ALEX: That's weird.

CAZ	You said you were sick.
SUSAN	No, I didn't—
EMMA	So we imagined it?
SUSAN	I said it was medical!
ALEX	What's the difference, Susan?
EMMA	Ohhh! I know! She had a boob job!
CAZ	(*smirking*) Clearly not.
ALEX	Don't be a bitch, Caz. And stop being so proud of your tits. It's pathetic.

Caz *pulls back, confused. Weren't they united against the new girl?*

ALEX	(*nicer*) Susan, I'm sorry, but you need to tell me. I can't afford to be sick this term. It's really important to me. So if you don't tell us, well... I'm going to have to ask Mr Bromley—
SUSAN	(*interrupts*) —I had an abortion.

A beat. Another beat. And then **Caz** *and* **Emma** *erupt, gleeful, scandalised.*

CAZ	Fucking HELL! I didn't expect that!
EMMA	(*shrieking*) An ABORTION?!
SUSAN	(*distressed*) Shhh! Keep your voice down!
CAZ	'Not that interesting,' she says! Just a casual abortion!
EMMA	So you have had sex!
CAZ	(*imitating*) 'Oh, it was nothing. You know; just an abortion!'
EMMA	I thought she was a lezzer!
ALEX	(*commanding*) Fuck's sake! Shut up, you two.

Surprised, **Emma** *and* **Caz** *shut up.* **Alex** *walks over to* **Susan** *and places a hand on her arm.* **Susan** *is shaking.*

ALEX	Ignore them. They're children. Emma's still a virgin.
EMMA	(*whining*) Alex!

ALEX   You're not crying, are you?

SUSAN   *(bravado)* No! No, I'm fine. It wasn't a big deal.

Alex *withdraws her hand from* **Susan's** *arm.*

ALEX   *(cold)* Wow. OK.

SUSAN   No, I didn't mean... I meant... it was... I...

Susan *trails off.*

ALEX   OK. Susan — sit down. Over here.

Caz *and* **Emma** *make space on the bed.* **Susan** *sits down in between them.*

ALEX   We won't tell anyone. *(to* Caz *and* Emma*)* Will we?

Caz *and* **Emma** *murmur agreement.*

ALEX   Because they'd jump on it. That's what they're like round here. They love a witch-hunt — don't they, Caz? Remember when you blew Toby and everyone found out? That was two years ago and they still go on about it. Don't they?

CAZ   Yeah.

EMMA   They make BJ faces behind her back.

CAZ   They do?

EMMA   And someone put raw hotdogs in her rucksack the other day.

ALEX   All right. That's enough. We don't want to scare her.

SUSAN   Please don't tell anyone.

ALEX   I just said we wouldn't, didn't I?

SUSAN   I just want to forget about it.

Alex *laughs.*

ALEX   You better learn to keep a secret, then. You've only been here five minutes and you've already blabbed!

CAZ (*mutters*) Showing off, prob'ly.

SUSAN (*quiet*) I wasn't.

Alex opens Susan's wardrobe and starts looking through her clothes.

ALEX It's fine, we tell each other everything here. It's what friends do. Share things.

Ooh, this is nice!

Alex pulls out one of Susan's tops and holds it against herself.

ALEX Can I?

Alex doesn't wait for the go-ahead; she's already changing into it.

ALEX What do you think?

CAZ Looks good.

EMMA Suits you.

ALEX Susan? What do you think?

A beat.

Susan gives a ragged smile.

SUSAN Looks better on you than me.

Alex smiles back, triumphant.

ALEX Thanks babe.

End of scene.

THE BEHOLDER

(Extract from play)

Written by

Hughie Shepherd-Cross

Hughie Shepherd-Cross is a playwright and comedy writer. His plays are full of absurd anecdotes, wordplay, and a lingering comic sadness. He has written three plays which have been performed at the Edinburgh Fringe, collaborated on various musical comedies, and is currently working with a group of young comedians on the London stand-up scene.

hughieshepherdcross@hotmail.com

SCENE 1

A chorus of city sounds: the flowing of the Thames, pub chatter, a tube train going through a tunnel. It settles on rain falling on a conservatory roof.

Blair and Marie sit in the conservatory.

BLAIR   You know, Marie, I'm beginning to think there's something going on in this city. I'm not sure what, but there's something going on. The sun's not setting the same, have you noticed that? It's far too vivid. The sun sets like it's putting it on, do you know what I mean? You see the people queuing along the bridge every time, with the wind blowing through their hair. Like they didn't used to. Like they used to perhaps on a Friday. There's something going on and I don't like it. The women, they look like they're off to somewhere. Every time I see them. Dressed up like they're off to somewhere. In the middle of the day, off to somewhere. No one's just going nowhere. Do you know what I mean? There's always something going on for them to go to and I don't like it. There's something going on I tell you.

MARIE   It's July, Blair, what the hell are you talking about? That's what's going on.

BLAIR   It's something more than that, I tell you. Our friends have got funnier.

MARIE   Huh?

BLAIR   Iona. She's a whole lot funnier than she ever was. And she's not just going through a good patch. It's like she's been given a whole new set of reflexes. Don't you see? Don't you find yourself laughing at Iona like you never have before. Like you've never noticed her before? And Jonathan, he's become much more personable.

MARIE   I don't know what to say. Can you accept that you might just be happy?

BLAIR   No. No way. There's something going on and I'm not happy about it.

MARIE   Well, then. Maybe it's just that you're in love.

BLAIR   Of course I'm in love, but that's got nothing to do with it. You know, I tell you something I've noticed, and I don't like it, it sends shivers down my spine. Since when was every tramp a poet? You noticed that? Maybe the poetry's not paying like it used to but there's something else going on, I tell you. It didn't used to be like this. You know I offer a chap a ploughman's the other day, guess what he says to me?

MARIE   That's very kind of you.

BLAIR   He says to me I can't live in a sandwich. That's the stuff of great verse. That's the stuff of legends, Marie. What's a man on the streets for if he can say something like that? He should be performing to the court. There's something going on in this city.

MARIE   There was a time when you'd spit at a man for saying something like that.

BLAIR   Exactly, there's something going on.

MARIE   What do you think's going on?

BLAIR   They're putting on a show.

MARIE   For who? *Pause*. You don't think they're putting on a show for you?

BLAIR   Not for me.

MARIE   Because I'm afraid to say, I care about you a lot, but I don't have that sort of power. No one does.

BLAIR   Not for me. I heard it at work. They're going through the department. Heard an 'all right, copper' on the stairs. Saw someone tip his cap on floor five. Soon they'll be phasing

	in the 'good day to you, sir's. I'm next, I tell you, I'm going to be indoctrinated. Given a bumbly walk and a tired looking uniform. Given a new set of jokes that I share with my colleagues. Updated idioms. Updated cultural palette. There's something going on I tell you.
MARIE	Who on earth would be doing this and why? You've got to think why anyone would want to do this?
BLAIR	They're not happy with the way this city's gone, you see. Lost its character. Gone all bland. Gone all grey. And there's visitors coming. Visitors from high up. Want to impress them. Give them a flavour. What it used to be.
MARIE	Who are these visitors, who are they?
BLAIR	Japan. They're ambassadors from Japan. There's something going on.
MARIE	Why do you keep on saying there's something going on if you're exactly sure of what is going on?
BLAIR	I can see it's already happened to you. I can see in your eyes. Your emotions are beautiful. They're charming. Like you're waving goodbye to me from a train station platform. Like your sadness is out of a catalogue.
MARIE	What are you trying to do to me?
BLAIR	You're doing it now.
MARIE	What the hell are you doing to me?
BLAIR	No one will notice. Everyone will forget. The crinkles will be ironed out. The gaps will be filled. It will seem just the same.

SCENE 2

The chorus returns: birds singing in a park, church bells ringing, the applause of a crowd. It settles on light city traffic.

Peter and Hodge sit on a roadside.

PETER	—and I was only asking for a smoke.
HODGE	—all he got was a pound of flour and a bottle of piss.

Blair enters, whistling and humming. As Peter and Hodge go on and on, Blair drifts in and out of enchantment.

BLAIR	Right, lads, time to move on.
PETER	Don't mind me, old copper.
HODGE	Don't mind me.
BLAIR	I'm afraid I can't do that. Up you get.
PETER	My old man was a marquess.
HODGE	My old man did nothing with his life.
PETER	But as it goes, I'm just a mark.
HODGE	He was a very successful Jainist.
PETER	Lost the rest on taxes.
HODGE	He never did a thing.
PETER	Wanted to marry a duchess. But as it went, he just married Dutch.
HODGE	Some folks get an indoor swimming pool.
PETER	They say, let's go Dutch, when they mean let's split it in half.
HODGE	We've got an outdoor sitting room.
PETER	But no one spares a thought for the half-Dutch.
BLAIR	What are you—
HODGE	It's by the Houses of Parliament.
PETER	It's the location we're paying for.
HODGE	You save a fortune on news.
BLAIR	I am not sure how all this is relevant, chaps. On you go.

PETER	I know half of the people in there.
HODGE	Their bottom half.
PETER	On a good year.
HODGE	In nineteen fifty-six.
BLAIR	I meant, on you go. Up you get, and on you go.
PETER	I once knew great men.
HODGE	I was never introduced.
PETER	Dylan Thomas was a friend of mine.
BLAIR	Really?
HODGE	I've lived a solitary life.
PETER	Delightful fellow.
HODGE	But who can hope to live two?
PETER	Extremely irritable at sunset.
HODGE	My old man lived three but did nothing with them.
PETER	And his get-well cards were depressing.
HODGE	My old mule lived three but did nothing at all.
PETER	I read a poem at his funeral. No one can remember it.
HODGE	Not even you.
BLAIR	How'd you chaps meet?
PETER	We were friends from a young age.
HODGE	I was his servant.
PETER	From a young age.
HODGE	I was his child servant.
PETER	And look where you are now. The top of the world!
HODGE	A pavement.
PETER	I had everything.
HODGE	I had nothing.
PETER	It was taken from me.
HODGE	And still, it was taken from me.

BLAIR	I'll need something more specific than that if you want to report—
PETER	If you're going to write a letter in blood, be sure what you're going to say.
HODGE	I water down my ink. Saves a few bob.
PETER	I was writing one to my step-mother. Passed out by the fourth draft.
HODGE	Got the idea off Joseph Turner.
PETER	She'd stolen my house.
HODGE	You leave anything inside?
PETER	A Monet, if you must know.
BLAIR	If you want to report anything then I can take you to the station, but it's time to be on your way.
HODGE	I once owned a Matisse. Might've been a placebo.
PETER	A reproduction.
HODGE	A placebo. I was subject to a trial on the effects of art on the uncivilised mind.
PETER	I knew a fella who was allergic to Cezannes.
HODGE	Just got a rash on my thighs.
PETER	Van Gogh makes me weep. Reminds me of my mother.
BLAIR	This is getting foolish now.
PETER	She found you on a crescent.
HODGE	On a waning crescent moon. Just a slither in the sky.
PETER	Regent's Crescent.
HODGE	Just a slither on the ground.
PETER	She found you in a dustbin.
HODGE	I don't like to talk about it.
PETER	A hopeless orphan.
HODGE	My parents were alive and well.
PETER	We all were once.

HODGE	We'd had our differences. I was independent.
PETER	You hadn't lived a year.
HODGE	They were going to the Himalayas.
PETER	They fished them out the Thames.
HODGE	They were going for a swim.
BLAIR	Christ.
PETER	My father took a shine to you.
HODGE	I shone his shoes.
PETER	It was a reciprocal arrangement.
HODGE	He made me shine till I could see my own face.
PETER	Which is torture with a face like that.
HODGE	I was sick on his shoes every morning.
PETER	The munter of Ealing.
HODGE	Who said that?
PETER	Everyone, behind your back.
HODGE	What were they doing there?
PETER	Avoiding your face.
HODGE	You're not the most handsome man in the world.
PETER	No, but he was a good friend of mine. School children would have to look at your face as a punishment.
HODGE	That's terribly cruel.
PETER	That's why it was banned. Had to start beating them instead.
HODGE	I've grown into my looks.
PETER	I got used to them.
HODGE	We became best friends.
PETER	In the evenings.
HODGE	If I could get off work on time.
PETER	I was his boss.
HODGE	I did the evenings unpaid.

PETER	We'd throw rocks by the river.
HODGE	The best days of my life.
PETER	I knew that better days lay ahead of me.
HODGE	Felt like they'd last forever.
PETER	I had to let him go.
HODGE	Left me in a gutter. No one even put up a fight.
PETER	My mother was ill.
BLAIR	Right lads, it seriously is time to move on.
PETER	The past's all we've got.
BLAIR	You've been here for three hours. It's time to move on.
HODGE	This pavement's all we've got.
BLAIR	Come on now.
PETER	My old man was a marquess.
BLAIR	I've heard the spiel, it's time to move on.

SCENE 3

The chorus returns. Leaves rustling in the wind. A tuba being practised. A lunatic preaching. It settles on the Thames.

Peter and Hodge stand by a river.

HODGE	I once knew a fella who skimmed a stone across the water and half the way back.
PETER	How'd he do that?
HODGE	No one knows. There was a thick mist upon the city. Some folks think it ricocheted off a pole. Some folks think his brother was on the other side.
PETER	I lost my first son to a thick mist.
HODGE	I met my first wife in a heavy fog.
PETER	When it rose he was a widely renowned stockbroker with a high standing in society.

HODGE	She didn't know I looked like this.
PETER	Never spoke to me again.
HODGE	She once told me she was leaving me forever and never coming back.
PETER	I was married to a tightrope walker. Told her instructor to cut her some slack.
HODGE	Returned fifteen minutes later with a pint of milk.
PETER	She fell to her death.
HODGE	We didn't know what the future held.
PETER	I was torn apart by grief until I found love again.
HODGE	She went to get her palms read.
PETER	It was the hardest weekend of my life.
HODGE	They were illegible. Died with no future and a meagre past.
PETER	Grief's a terrible thing.
HODGE	I lost a friend to a gutter fire.
PETER	I lost a friend to a chimney flood.
HODGE	I had a friend that went missing piece by piece.
PETER	I had a friend that woke up one morning, read his own obituary, was so pleased with it that he hanged himself.
HODGE	But you get over it.
PETER	Turns out it was just about a fella with the same name.
HODGE	What was it?
PETER	Clement Atlee.
HODGE	I knew a fella who found out he was the illegitimate son of a wrongfully convicted murderer.
PETER	I once knew the namesakes to great men.
HODGE	Drove him mad.
PETER	Isambard Kingdom Brunel was a friend of mine.

GENDER ROLLS: 'THE PURPLE DRESS'

(Extract from film)

Written by

Alex Viney

Alex Viney is a writer interested in playing with genres, tropes and perspectives, as well as gender and identity, the latter two of which she explores on her podcast, 'Apple Time Podcast'. She is currently working on the screenplay 'Gender Rolls' (her submission is an extract), which examines how games and play can lead us to internal revelations and forge lasting bonds with others.

Podcast can be found at tinyurl.com/AppleTimePod.

alexviney@gmail.com

INT. THE REALM OF URBEMSULA, THE KING'S PALACE — NIGHT

A white and gold palace wall, with a painting of a knight in full armour standing to attention hanging on it.

With a THUD and a CRACK, AZOHAR THE COURT WIZARD is thrown against the wall, knocking the painting down with him. Thin, silver hair coated with blood, pale, dressed in robes. He looks worse for wear.

An axe-blade appears at Azohar's neck and he presses himself flat against the wall, whimpering.

                    AZOHAR
     P-p-please! No! I'll do anything
     that you—

TERRENCE, a towering and buff Minotaur with half-singed fur in a tailcoat tuxedo, holding the axe, interrupts.

                    TERRENCE
     Eat a dick.

He shoves the axe forward. It slices cleanly through Azohar's neck, and his surprised expression rolls to the ground.

The axe cuts through the canvas of the painting and lodges into the wall.

Terrence smirks.

A beat.

                    FLORIN (O.C.)
     What the *fuck*, Terry?

                    TERRENCE
     Huh?

FLORIN, a young man in immaculate blue and white religious robes, stares at Terrence with wide glowing orange eyes.

                    FLORIN
     We were gonna question him!

                    TERRENCE
     What?

                    FLORIN
          We're never gonna find out who
          ordered the raid now!

Terrence lowers his axe.

                    TERRENCE
          Hmm. No.

Florin puts his face in his hands.

                    TERRENCE
          You have healing magic.

                    FLORIN
          Yeah, I've got 'Cure Wounds', not
          fucking 'Reattach Head'!

                    TERRENCE
          Right.

A beat.

                    TERRENCE
          It's *kind of* a wound.

Florin pinches the bridge of his nose.

Florin looks to the ceiling.

                    FLORIN
              (upwards)
          Would that work?

From above, from nowhere, from everywhere:

                    VOICE OF MARIE (V.O.)
              (a sigh)
          Sure. Roll a nat 20.

                    FLORIN
          Fine. Tish, hold the head in place.

TISH, a nervous-looking elf in a lilac ball gown, gawks at the idea.

                    TISH
          We're definitely not being invited
          to the next gala.

FLORIN
          That's a given.

He crouches down next to Azohar's body, the forming pool of blood staining his robes.

He waves over Tish, who also kneels, grabbing the severed head and holding it in place at the bleeding neck.

Tish leans over to Florin.

                    TISH
          (whispering)
          This counts as a Help Action, right?

Florin thinks for a moment.

Florin and Tish both look upwards.

                    VOICE OF MARIE (V.O.)
          (another sigh)
          Fine. Both roll.

Tish and Florin both focus on the body in front of them.

Florin places his hands on the body and they start to glow.

Next to each of Tish and Florin, an ever-changing flashing number appears, quickly and randomly cycling through 1—20.

The cycling slows down. Florin's number stops at 18.

He scowls.

                    FLORIN
          Shit. So close. How'd you do?

Tish sheepishly avoids his gaze. A floating '1' above her shoulder.

                    TERRENCE
          Did it—

The head in Tish's hand starts screaming.

Tish starts screaming.

                    AZOHAR'S HEAD
          AHHH! PAAAAIIIINNN! I'M IN PAIN! SO
          MUCH PAIN! MIND-BOGGLING! UNENDING!

>   PAIN! I WAS DEAD AND AT PEACE AND
>   NOW I'M ALIVE AND IN PAIN! AHHHH!!
>   SOMEBODY—

Azohar's screaming is cut off as he dies for the second time in three minutes.

A beat.

> TISH
> We're definitely going to Hell.

> TERRENCE
> Oh yeah.

INT. THE REAL WORLD, MARIE'S BEDROOM – AFTERNOON

Light blue walls, a big bed, oak wardrobes and a massive window letting in light. Heavy metal band posters: Powerwolf, Alestorm, etc. Another poster of a red dragon breathing fire upon a mountaintop.

Morgan sits on the floor, leaning against the wall beneath the window, using a thick textbook as a support as he fills out a maths worksheet. His hair has grown since we last saw him and looks shaggier.

Beside him is his rucksack, across from him is a stack of papers and textbooks, and a beanbag with an imprint where Marie was sat moments ago.

Now, Marie is stood on the other side of her room, rifling through her closet.

Both are still in their school uniforms, but have loosened their ties.

> MORGAN
> What did you get for 2 a part 4?

> MARIE
> (pronouncing the letters)
> Part I V?

> MORGAN
> Yeah.

MARIE
Haven't got to it yet. Just finished
part I I I.

MORGAN
Part 3?

MARIE
Yeah.

Morgan frowns. Chews the end of his pen.

MORGAN
I'm struggling with it.

MARIE
Give me a sec and I'll come back,
just looking for — *This!*

Marie pulls something from her cupboard.

It's a ball gown very similar to the one Tish wore in the previous scene.

MARIE
This is what I was thinking of when
I described Tish's dress during the
last session!

Morgan looks up.

MORGAN
Why do you have that?

MARIE
I did LARP last summer.

MORGAN
The thing where people in fields hit
each other with foam swords?

Marie nods.

She gestures to the dress and grins.

MARIE
What do you think?

                    MORGAN
          I think I'm reassessing how cool I
          thought you were when we first met.

                    MARIE
          Fuck off. I am cool.

Morgan grins.

                    MORGAN
          Right. 'Course.

Marie hangs the dress up on the outside of her wardrobe and
returns to the floor, lying forward on the bean bag and going
back to her worksheet.

                    MARIE
          Oh — I lied, I have done part 4.

                    MORGAN
          Did you get 16.7?

Marie shakes her head.

                    MARIE
          13.2.

                    MORGAN
          Bollocks. Where'd I go wrong?

                    MARIE
          Show.

Morgan turns his worksheet to show Marie.

She taps a part of his working with her pen.

                    MARIE
          You *divide* by 4, not multiply.

                    MORGAN
          What?

He spins the sheet back around. Squints at it.

                    MORGAN
          Thanks.

He crosses out his previous working and redoes the question.

Marie starts scribbling answers onto her own worksheet.

Morgan chews the end of his pen. He looks up at the dress hanging on Marie's wardrobe, for the first time giving proper attention to it.

It's a medieval gown with puffy shoulders and a corset-body. Trimmed with pieces of lace. A centuries-past brand of beautiful.

Morgan takes the pen out of his mouth. His attention is now fully on the dress.

A breath catches in Morgan's throat.

Marie hears this and looks up at Morgan.

She follows the eyeline of his dilated pupils.

>   MARIE
> You like it?

>   MORGAN
> Hmm? Pardon?

Marie grins.

>   MARIE
> You like the dress?

>   MORGAN
> Looks expensive.

A beat. Then, completely casually:

>   MARIE
> Want to try it on?

Morgan chokes on air.

>   MORGAN
> What!?

Marie shrugs.

>   MARIE
> We're probably about the same size.

Morgan pales.

He gulps, his heart racing.

>   MORGAN
> I — umm — well —

Clammy hands tighten their hold on Morgan's textbook.

After a deep breath, Morgan clears his throat and forces his attention away from the dress.

>   MORGAN
> No. Why would I?

Marie rolls her eyes.

>   Marie
> Oh *go on*.

>   MORGAN
> Pardon?

>   MARIE
>   (teasing)
> You'll feel very *pretty* I'm sure.

Morgan's throat tightens when Marie says 'pretty'.

>   MORGAN
> No thanks.

>   MARIE
> Please?

>   MORGAN
>   (firm)
> Leave it.

>   MARIE
> Oh come on.

>   MORGAN
> I'm serious.

>   MARIE
> Don't be a pussy, I know you—

>   MORGAN
>   (face red, exploding)
> JUST FUCK OFF! OK?

The room rings silent for a beat after the shout.

As soon as he raises his voice, Morgan regrets it.

Marie's eyes are wide.

Her shock turns into an offended scowl.

                    MARIE
Fine. Sorry I said anything.

                    MORGAN
Marie, I—

                    MARIE
I said it's fine. Let's just finish the work.

Morgan watches her block him off entirely and go back to working on her worksheet.

The only sound is the scratching of pen on paper.

Morgan looks up at the dress.

He frowns at it.

He shakes his head and returns to his own worksheet.

THERE'S A HOLE IN MY BUCKET

(A self-contained microdrama)

Written by

Alexander Wiseman

Alexander Wiseman is a playwright and occasional actor based in Norwich and West Sussex. He has had several award-winning plays put on at venues in Norwich, and his undergraduate dissertation, *Philip I*, was the runner-up for the 2021 Snoo Wilson Scriptwriting Prize.

xander.wiseman@btinternet.com

A lush garden in the morning — flower beds, herbs, vines, vegetable patches.

ROD (mid-30s) stands at a large, metal water pump in the centre. He pumps away, and water dribbles.

APHRA (mid-30s) sits on an uncomfortable stool, bending down to hold a bucket under the spout — however the bucket never seems to fill at all.

They both look tired and aching, but they carry on (and don't stop unless otherwise stated).

About 30 seconds.

ROD   This isn't fun anymore.

APHRA   Was it ever?

ROD   Kinda. It's a good workout at least.

APHRA   For you, maybe. It's just killing my back.

ROD   Quit yer whining, you've got the easy job by far.

A few moments.

                Why do your parents have to care so much about all this anyway?

APHRA   All old people care about their gardens.

ROD   My folks don't.

APHRA   What?

ROD   They don't even have a garden; you've been round, you remember.

APHRA   Your parents are farmers, Rod.

ROD   Yeah? And they don't have a garden.

APHRA   They have acres and acres of garden!

ROD   They prefer to call the land their 'office.'

APHRA   OK, but do they care about the land?

ROD: Well, yeah, but it's not the same though, is it? It's their job.

APHRA: Fine. Fine, OK.

ROD: Don't do that, Aphra, come on.

APHRA: What? I'm agreeing with you. I'm saying you have made a valid point and I am recognising it and conceding defeat.

ROD: Oh, stop it.

APHRA: Stop what? Agreeing with you? Being on your side? If you insist, I'm sure you'd love th—

ROD: OK OK, I'm sorry, I'm sorry. OK? Ignore me.

Old people do tend to care about their gardens, you're right, I was being silly.

This is just tiring me out, y'know.

APHRA: Yeah. It's OK.

ROD: Why d'you think that is? That old folk care about gardening?

APHRA: I don't know. Something about being close to death wanting you to surround yourself with life. Maybe it makes them feel as if they can still have an effect on things. Maybe because they're bored, I don't know.

We'll find out one day, I suppose.

ROD: You wanna know what I think this is all about?

APHRA: I struggle to ever know what you think, darling.

ROD: I think that your parents have buggered off and left us here, tending their garden, getting hot and sweaty, to make us feel oh so sorry for them. We struggle and toil over this whole place; pulling weeds, clipping bushes, uprooting and replanting every veggie in a ratatouille, watering everything equipped with a single bucket — and

	we think: 'Oh, oh poor souls. This is tiring us out, but they've got to do this every day. Poor old things. We should offer to come round more and help out.' But I'm not gonna fall for it, not a chance. Cos I know, I know for sure that they've gotta have a gardener, or someone who comes round and helps. There's no way they do this all themselves. Your dad's on his, what, third hip? Your mum's half-blind, for God's sake. So they're not gonna get me with their little scheme, no chance.
APHRA	Or, and hear me out here, Rod, they were going on holiday and wanted us to house-sit. And what's wrong with us coming to visit more often? We really should.
ROD	It's a two-hour drive!
APHRA	They're my parents! And they don't have any 'little schemes,' please.
ROD	They always have some reason, some ulterior motive, for doing shit. D'you remember when we were here for Christmas with Del and Fi—
APHRA	... To spend Christmas with my family yeah.
ROD	—and they insisted that instead of getting them anything that we should donate to some charity for whales in their name?
APHRA	And?
ROD	Who does that? Who gets people to donate to a charity in their name? Why try and take the credit? They're not exactly in dire financial straits.
APHRA	It was a nice gesture, Rod.
ROD	I don't get it.
APHRA	No, well you wouldn't. Nice gestures are foreign to you, aren't they? You *just don't get* them.

ROD — Nice gestures are never *just* nice gestures though, are they?

APHRA — Why not?

ROD — People do nice gestures for other people so that they'll get something in return.

You gift a bouquet of flowers to a partner; you expect sex or something. You make someone dinner; you expect them to make dinner for you in the future. You do a favour for someone; you expect them to do a favour for you, they owe you one.

APHRA — So you just don't bother.

ROD — Well I make an exception with you, of course.

APHRA — Oh, you do?

ROD — Yeah.

I do nice things for you, right?

APHRA — Mmm.

ROD — Do I?

APHRA — Yes, Rod, you do. I appreciate it.

ROD — Good.

APHRA — Although I can't remember the last time you got me flowers.

ROD — You're surrounded by flowers right now! Take your pick, it's not like your folks'll notice.

APHRA — That's not the point though, Rod, is it?

There's no thought, there's no effort in that, is there?

ROD — OK, OK, I'll get you some flowers.

APHRA — That's— argh.

ROD — What?

APHRA — It's not about the fucking flowers, Rod, it's—

ROD — Why are we talking about flowers then?

APHRA   It's about me being... I just want to know that you...

APHRA notices something in the bucket, fixates on it.

ROD   Just want to know that I what?

A few moments.

APHRA slowly gets up and backs away from the bucket.

ROD stops pumping.

               What is it?

APHRA	There's a hole in the bucket.
ROD	You're kidding.
APHRA	There's a big fuck-off hole in the fucking bucket.

ROD goes round and looks into the bucket.

ROD	Fuck's sake, Aphra, how'd you only notice that now?
APHRA	I— I—
ROD	I've been pumping on this bloody thing for ages!
APHRA	I know, I— I'm sorry!
ROD	Christ, love. Jesus.
APHRA	I'm sorry, I didn't know.
ROD	Why on earth do your folks have one bucket, and why does it have a goddamn hole in it?
APHRA	I'm sorry.
ROD	It's not your fault. It's probably part of their scheme, I told you.
APHRA	I should've known. I should've looked.

APHRA picks up the bucket and holds it close to her.

               I don't know how I didn't notice.

She sits on the floor, legs splayed.

ROD   It's OK.

APHRA   I should've noticed. It was right in front of me. It was my job.

ROD   Your job was to sit there and look pretty, and you were doing that fantastically.

APHRA   How did I not notice?

ROD   You were distracted. I was distracting you, that's all. I should've told you to check the bucket.

APHRA   It's not your responsibility to tell me to check whether my bucket has a fucking hole in it or not! *The* bucket.

            It's *my* responsibility. It's nothing to do with you.

ROD   It's everything to do with me; I'm the one doing the pumping. We're here doing this together, both equally responsible.

APHRA   You were doing your part just fine, and I—

            I just feel so stupid.

ROD sits next to APHRA, takes one of her hands and holds it.

ROD   You're not stupid. Of course not. It's not your fault.

APHRA   How the fuck're we gonna water all these fucking plants now?

ROD   They'll survive until your parents get back just fine, I'm sure.

            There's not much of anything we can do.

APHRA takes her hand back and clings together to the bucket.

ROD   Give that thing here.

ROD goes to take the bucket from APHRA, but she pushes his hand away.

APHRA   Don't touch it. It's mine.

A few moments.

APHRA I was actually enjoying it.

ROD What?

APHRA The whole process. Not just getting the water, but everything else. The gardening. Weeding and rearranging. Cutting back and prepping everything for the next season. It was nice. It felt nice.

And we were good at it, up until now, we worked well together.

I was thinking that maybe, when we got home, we could start working on our garden — what little of a garden we have, y'know. I've always been embarrassed by the state of our front garden compared to the Chelsea Flower Show-level stuff that everyone else on our road seems to have. We've just got a dusty pit. But, no, I don't want to because I'm embarrassed, I want to because I want to. I want to create and craft something beautiful, or try to, create some life and have some fun doing it, have fun with you, instead of waiting until we're old and bored.

I was thinking that we could do that... But if I can't even notice that a bucket has a gaping hole in it then there's no chance, there's no point.

ROD Of course there's a chance. We could... figure something out.

APHRA I'm sorry, my love. You're probably relieved.

ROD You have absolutely nothing to apologise for.

OK?

We could get someone in to help us. I've got a gardener friend who owes me a favour.

APHRA   That'd be even worse. Everyone looking and seeing that we couldn't do it ourselves.

ROD   Lots of people get help, it's not abnormal.

APHRA   Rod, please, just—

ROD   It'll be OK, we'll just, well we'll—

APHRA   Rod.

                    Just let me be sad for the moment.

ROD   ... Right.

A few moments.

ROD tries to put his arm around APHRA, but she shifts away.

ROD   I'll just... uh...

ROD gets up and begins to meander off.

ROD   I don't know what you want from me, Aphra.

He exits.

A few moments.

APHRA looks into the bucket.

Eventually, she exits.

LIE DETECTORS

(Extract from film)

Written by

Yu Ching Wong

Yu Ching Wong is a writer from Hong Kong. She won two creative grants awarded by YMCA and The University of Hong Kong in 2018 and published her short stories at the Hong Kong Book Fair in the same year. She is interested in exploring different forms of storytelling.

natw@connect.hku.hk

INT. POLICE STATION CORRIDOR — THURSDAY AFTERNOON

Lawrence Brown (35) is on his way to the interrogation room. His colleague, Thomas Taylor (40), happens to come out of the room and bumps into him.

LAWRENCE
You all right, mate?

THOMAS
Not too bad.

LAWRENCE
How was the interrogation? Did it go well?

THOMAS
No, it was difficult. The guy was tight-lipped. A lot of the things he said seemed pretty dodgy.

LAWRENCE
He's in good hands. See what I've got with me.

Lawrence flashes his lie detector. It is a small device with a glossy black surface which gives out a tiny green speck of light.

THOMAS
You're going to rely on this thing again?

LAWRENCE
Well, I tried it on a guy two days ago and it was brilliant. Besides, David said it has worked very well in his experience.

THOMAS
(Nods) Sounds good. I gotta go now. John is looking for me. Good luck!

LAWRENCE
Cheers!

Thomas gives Lawrence a quick pat on the shoulder and walks away. Lawrence slips the lie detector device into his pocket and enters the interrogation room.

CUT TO:

INT. SUPERMARKET, FRUIT SECTION NEAR THE ENTRANCE — THURSDAY EVENING (THREE HOURS LATER)

Lawrence enters and takes a basket at the entrance. He is tired from work and looks sleepy. He walks straight ahead to the fruit section and runs into his neighbour, Mrs Smith.

          MRS SMITH
Hey, Mr Brown! Good to see you here!

How are you?

          LAWRENCE
I'm good, thank you!

The lie detector buzzes. A beep. Lawrence starts at the sound of the device. He reaches into his pocket and realises that he is carrying the lie detector.

          LAWRENCE (CONT'D)
Well, I mean not too bad.

Work has been quite busy lately. How are you?

          MRS SMITH
I'm fine, thank you. I'm doing my last-minute shopping to prepare for dinner tonight.

          LAWRENCE
You've got a lot of food in your trolley. Is there a celebration tonight?

          MRS SMITH
Yes, Matt and I are celebrating our 10th anniversary tonight.

          LAWRENCE
Lovely! By the way, I haven't seen Mr Smith much recently. How has he been?

          MRS SMITH
He's very busy with work at the moment. He has been travelling quite a lot recently but he always tries to make time for me whenever he can.

A beep. The lie detector buzzes in Lawrence's pocket. Mrs Smith notices the noise. She looks puzzled but carries on.

MRS SMITH (CONT'D)
We are both doing quite well, thank you.

Pause. A beep again. Lawrence reaches into his pocket and clutches the device, hoping to minimise the vibrations and sounds it makes.

LAWRENCE
Ah, that's... that's very nice! I mean... good to know.

MRS SMITH
(puzzled) If you don't mind me asking, is there a sound coming from your pocket? I keep hearing a low buzzing sound.

LAWRENCE
Oh yes! Oh sorry, it's my phone. I think I've got a call...

Lawrence fishes out his mobile phone and pretends that he sees a missed call on the screen.

LAWRENCE (CONT'D)
This is embarrassing but I'm really happy to see you here. I'd better go now, see you around and Happy Anniversary!

Lawrence quickly grabs a bag of oranges and hurries off, holding the lie detector in a tight grasp. He gazes at the device and sees that the green light keeps flashing non-stop.

INT. SUPERMARKET, BAKERY COUNTER — THURSDAY EVENING

Lawrence leaves quickly to avoid further embarrassing himself. He comes to the bakery counter and sees a mother and her teenage daughter chatting. He immediately slides the device back into his pocket.

MOTHER
Why were you so late last night?

> TEENAGE DAUGHTER
> I spent the whole day working in the library. It's the exam season, Mum.

A beep and a buzz. Lawrence rummages in his pocket for the device. Once he grabs hold of it, he clutches it firmly in his palm while he searches for the on-off switch with his fingers.

> MOTHER
> Are you sure you didn't sneak out to meet Jonathan again?

> TEENAGE DAUGHTER
> Mum, I'm telling you the truth. I have been spending a lot of time with Susan lately. I go to her house to study with her all the time and I haven't seen Jonathan for nearly three weeks!

A beep and a buzz. Lawrence immediately turns around to avoid facing the mother and the daughter directly. He finally figures out where the on-off switch is.

> MOTHER
> All right, I'm just worried about you. Dad and I can come and give you a lift if you can't catch a bus. Give us a ring next time, OK?

> TEENAGE DAUGHTER
> All right, Mum. Don't worry. I've just been working hard.

A beep. The device buzzes vigorously. The mother looks alert. Lawrence flicks the on-off switch frantically in his pocket.

> MOTHER
> What's that sound?

The mother and her daughter look around and finally stare at Lawrence suspiciously. He is the only person standing in the immediate vicinity.

> LAWRENCE
> Oh! Sorry, it's my phone. Must be in high demand!

Lawrence feigns nonchalance and forces a few laughs. He takes out his mobile phone and shakes his head, acting as if he is slightly frustrated with it. The mother nods politely while the teenage daughter keeps staring at him dubiously. Lawrence grabs a loaf of bread and hurries away as soon as the daughter stops looking.

INT. SUPERMARKET, FROZEN FOOD SECTION – THURSDAY EVENING

Lawrence comes to the frozen food section. He sees a man in a smart suit talking loudly on his phone right beside a freezer containing ready meals. In the meantime, he keeps fumbling with the on-off switch of the device.

>MAN
>Don't worry, James. Mr Richardson is apparently very happy with our proposal. I think we'll be able to close the deal in three months.

A beep. The device buzzes.

>LAWRENCE
>(whispers to himself)
>Damn it.

>MAN
>Yes, yes, everything's all good. I've got things in check. Next week, I'll have a meeting with Sam's team to confirm the expenses. He is cool with our proposed schedule. No worries at all.

A beep. The device buzzes again. The man frowns and turns around. He shoots Lawrence a doubtful glance. Lawrence takes out his mobile phone, points at it and mouths the words to the man in suit.

>LAWRENCE
>Excuse me, it's my phone.

Lawrence has been clutching the device the whole time and he can feel sweat in his palm. He keeps flicking the on-off switch but fails to shut down the device. He can not stand the discomfort and embarrassment any further. He opens the freezer door and quickly grabs a few pasta boxes, then heads towards the checkout.

INT. SUPERMARKET, CHECKOUT — THURSDAY EVENING

Lawrence loosens his grip on the device as he is ready to pay. He places his basket onto the tray and runs his items under the scanners of the self-checkouts. The lie detector slips out of his pocket as he bends over to transfer his items from the basket to his bag. It falls into a dark corner behind the bin collecting unwanted receipts.

> SELF-CHECKOUT
> VOICE ASSISTANT
> Please scan your loyalty card to
> earn points with your shopping.

Lawrence takes out his card and scans it without noticing he has dropped his device accidentally. He looks slightly flustered.

> SELF-CHECKOUT
> VOICE ASSISTANT
> Thank you for shopping with us.
> Do you need a bag?

> LAWRENCE
> No.

> SELF-CHECKOUT
> VOICE ASSISTANT
> Thank you and have a nice day! Shop
> Corp. is happy to serve you.

ANGLE ON the lie detector. The device gives out a faint beep and a low buzz behind the bin.

> LAWRENCE
> (Sighs)
> Well, at least the machines are
> sincere.

Lawrence grabs his food and leaves the supermarket. ANGLE ON the device which keeps flashing a green light in the dark corner.

Acknowledgements

This anthology contains work written by the 2021 cohort of UEA's MA Creative Writing: Scriptwriting. We are very grate- ful for the support of the UEA School of Literature, Drama and Creative Writing in partnership with Egg Box Publishing, part of UEA Publishing Project, Ltd., without whom this anthology would not have been possible.

We would like to thank Steve Waters, Molly Naylor, Ben Musgrave, Sian Evans, Timberlake Wertenbaker, and Ian Gonoude for their tutoring and support over the past year.

Huge thanks to Shannon Clinton-Copeland and Nathan Hamilton at the UEA Publishing Project, Emily Benton and Sarah Gooderson for their help managing, designing and proofreading this anthology. Thanks also to our Scriptwriting editors Hughie Shepherd-Cross, David McCabe, Alex Viney, and Dan Clark.

Lastly, of course, massive thanks to our fellow course-mates for the feedback and communal spirit over the often challenging year gone by.

UEA MA Creative Writing Anthologies: Script Writing

First published by Egg Box Publishing, 2021
Part of the UEA Publishing Project Ltd.

International © retained by individual authors

This book is sold subject to the condition that it shall not, by way of trade or otherwise, be lent, resold, hired out, stored in a retrieval system, or otherwise circulated without the publisher's prior consent in any form of binding or cover other than that in which it is published and without a similar condition including this condition being imposed on the subsequent purchaser.

A CIP record for this book is available from the British Library
Printed and bound in the UK by Imprint Digital

Designed by Emily Benton Book Design
emilybentonbookdesign.co.uk

Proofread by Sarah Gooderson

Distributed by NBN International
10 Thornbury Road
Plymouth
PL6 7PP
+44 (0)1752 202 301
e.cservs@nbninternational.com

ISBN 978-1-913861-27-8